THE SHAMBHALA GUIDE TO KENDO

THE
SHAMBHALA GUIDE TO
KENDO

Minoru Kiyota

SHAMBHALA

Boston & London

2002

SHAMBHALA PUBLICATIONS, INC.
Horticultural Hall
300 Massachusetts Avenue
Boston, Massachusetts 02115
www.shambhala.com

Previously published under the title *Kendō*
Published by arrangement with Kegan Paul Limited, London, England

© 1995, 2002 by Minoru Kiyota

9 8 7 6 5 4 3 2 1

FIRST SHAMBHALA EDITION

Printed in the United States of America

⊗ This edition is printed on acid-free paper that meets
the American National Standards Institute Z39.48 Standard.

Distributed in the United States by Random House, Inc.,
and in Canada by Random House of Canada Ltd

ART CREDITS
Art on page 2 by Stefan Geissler. Art on page 3 is from the
program announcement of the Sixth Annual Midwest
Kendo Federation Tournament. Photos appearing on pages 5, 10, 11, 12, 13, 14, 20
are by Emannuel Voyiziakis.

Library of Congress Cataloging-in-Publication Data

Kiyota, Minoru, 1923–
    The Shambhala guide to Kendo / Minoru Kiyota.— 1st Shambhala ed.
       p.   cm.
    Includes bibliographical references and index.
    ISBN 1-57062-927-7
    1. Kendo.   I. Title.

GV1142 .K595   2002
796.86—dc21

2001049088

Contents

Preface

KENDO IS THE MODERN version of Japanese swordsmanship. In 1964, Dr. Gordon Warner, a respected kendo practitioner, published an excellent manual of kendo techniques called *This Is Kendo.* In 1991, Hiroshi Ozawa, also a respected kendo practitioner, published *Kendo: The Definitive Guide.* Furthermore, in 1997, Karl F. Friday and Seki Humitake published *Legacies of the Sword,* an excellent treatment of the historical development of schools of kendo. Not wanting to repeat what these writers have said, I have chosen to focus on kendo's philosophical infrastructure and its potential contributions to personal growth. The purpose of this work is, therefore, to describe the discipline of kendo cultivated by the samurai in medieval and premodern Japan and to show the relevance of that discipline today. Discipline in the context of this work refers to the ways and means used to destroy the ego and to realize vision beyond that dictated by the ego. Ego refers to the agent that makes the self the measuring stick of the world.

The term *kendo* was used as early as the seventeenth century, although popular usage began sometime after the Meiji Restoration (1868), the period signaling Japan's emergence as a modern state. Literally, the term means "the way of the sword." It refers to a way of life that embodies the discipline acquired through kendo practice.

But even before the seventeenth century, terms other than *kendo* were used, such as *heiho, kenjitsu, kenpo, gekken,* each expressing a different nuance of meaning particular to the time. In this work, to avoid confusion, the term *swordsmanship* is employed when *kendo* is used in a general way. *Kendo* itself is used in two categories, classical and modern kendo, although these categorical descriptions are ignored when the historical context in which the term is used is apparent.

Classical kendo was influenced by Buddhism, Confucianism, and Shinto, but this work as a rule limits its discussion to Buddhism. This is because I consider Buddhism to be the most convenient vehicle to describe classical kendo philosophically. But although it deals with the Buddhist philosophical infrastructure of kendo, it is not designed for specialists in Buddhist philosophy. It describes the implementation of that philosophy on kendo, which I consider a form of popular culture. Although I treat kendo as popular culture, it is not designed for specialists in Japanese history. It briefly describes the historical circumstances that led to this popular culture at a particular period.

This work is divided into five chapters. Chapter 1 introduces kendo, identifies basic kendo concepts, and briefly interprets them within the framework of Buddhist thought. Chapter 2 is doctrinal. Here two schools of classical kendo—Katori-ryu (*ryu* means school), influenced by Shingon Buddhist thought, and Yagyu-ryu, influenced by Zen—are selected for examination. Chapter 3 provides the necessary historical background and, based on that background, discusses the development of kendo in two distinct periods: the Warring States period and the Tokugawa period (which is subdivided into early, middle, and late periods), the entire period spanning the early fifteenth to the late nineteenth centuries. The episodes discussed here are those of historical personalities, but many of the episodes themselves were most likely created during the last 150 years.

Chapter 4 deals with the implementation of discipline cultivated in classical kendo in medieval and premodern Japan. The way of life resulting from this discipline is referred to as *bushido* (*bushi* means "samurai," and *do* means "way of life"). Bushido was codified as early as the twelfth century but was not institutionalized until the seventeenth century. This chapter provides a historical contextualization and categorical interpretation of the major themes of bushido. It concludes by critically examining Nitobe Inazo's *Bushido: The Soul of Japan*, one of the very few comprehensive works on bushido published in English in 1900. Chapter 5 deals with the modern period. It critically evaluates kendo and bushido, describes a shifting value concept seen in the movement from classical to modern kendo, and presents ways and means to integrate martial and liberal arts in order to promote personal growth.

An annotated, selected list of references, of both Japanese and English publications, plus a glossary of technical terms are included. Japanese has been romanized according to the Hepburn system and Chinese by the Wade-Giles system. Family names precede given names, according to the Japanese tradition. But in this work, many samurai are identified by their first names after the full name is given. I have done this because many samurai treated in this work are popular personalities and are better known by their first names. For example, Miyamoto Musashi (Musashi being the first name) is better known as Musashi. Names of modern Japanese are rendered in the traditional manner, that is, family name first. Diacritics for Japanese and Sanskrit terms have been omitted.

I am grateful to the following persons whose instruction and/or friendship stimulated me to prepare this work: the late Takano Hiromasa, one of the greatest kendo masters of the contemporary period, who transmitted the Nakanish school of Ono-ha Itto-ryu and who introduced me to kendo many decades ago; to the late Professor Yuki Reimon of Tokyo University, under whom I continued my training while a graduate student at that university; and to Otake Risuke, the present headmaster of the Katori-ryu (classical kendo), who provided me with frequent instruction. I am also grateful to Dr. Julia Brown, Department of Kinesiology, University of Wisconsin–Madison (retired in 1994), for allowing me to first teach kendo as a part of the department's curriculum in 1989.

This work is a revised edition of my previous work on kendo first published in 1995. I am grateful to Beth Frankl, associate editor of Shambhala Publications, for providing me the opportunity to revise it.

Minoru Kiyota
University of Wisconsin–Madison

THE SHAMBHALA GUIDE TO KENDO

1
What Is Kendo?

Kendo and Sport

MODERN KENDO EQUIPMENT includes the *shinai*, a split bamboo stick just under four feet long (fig. 1), and the *bogu*, a set of light armor (fig. 2). The object in kendo combat is to deliver a strike or thrust with the shinai to prescribed targets on the bogu: the *men* (head), including the forehead and the right and left sides; the right and left sides of the *kote* (forearm); the right and left sides of the *do* (torso); and the *tsuki* (throat). Sometimes a thrust to the chest is also permitted. A strike or thrust is counted only when accompanied by speed, force, accuracy, physical coordination, and concentration.

With its special equipment and precisely defined rules, kendo fits the modern definition of a sport—a structured human activity[1] carried out in leisure time for the purpose of recreating the human personality. Leisure-time activities are those in which coercion is absent and that bring about a change of attitude in minds ordinarily focused on making a living.[2] The purpose of kendo is to enhance physical and mental growth. But kendo is different from other martial arts. For example, judo, karate, and aikido may have a certain value as weaponless forms of self-defense, but kendo requires a shinai, or for that matter a sword, something not normally carried on

1

Figure 1. Shinai

city streets. Kendo is basically designed to perfect the kind of discipline necessary to cultivate alertness, speed of action, and, most important of all, direct cognition. All these qualities are required to
cope with the flashing attacks of an opponent's shinai in the course
of intense combat practice. These qualities require concentration
rather than physical strength. Thus, kendo can be practiced by the
young and old, male and female.

Although kendo is a sport, it does have one major aspect that
differentiates it from Western sports: classical kendo developed
under actual battlefield conditions where life and death were at
stake, and under the influence of Buddhism.

FIGURE 2. Bogu

Mushin: An Altered State of Consciousness

When a samurai faced his opponent, sword drawn, fear was inevitably aroused. What was the source of this fear? The opponent? The sword that was thrust toward him? No. Fear is created by one's own mind. One must conquer the fear within oneself before one can conquer the opponent. How does the kendo practitioner do that?

The conscious mind gives rise to the ego. The ego is that aspect of the mind that takes the self as the measuring stick of the world and ultimately seeks self-preservation. It is the ego that breeds fear. Under this circumstance, the most effective move to make is an all-out "go-for-broke" attack, which is referred to as a *sutemi* (literally "body-abandoning") attack. It is in this kind of an attack—an attack in which there is no intrusion of the ego-based intellect—that a kendo practitioner is apt to discover *mushin.*

Mushin* is a term that D. T. Suzuki, the Zen master who made the term *Zen* a part of the Western vocabulary, translated as the "mind of no-mind."[3] Simply put, it refers to an altered state of conscious-ness, a state of mind freed from an ego-clouded vision that cannot be swayed by external distractions. This state of mind is called the true self. Of course, mushin is realized in many Western sports as well, for example, baseball, basketball, and swimming. But kendo is unique because it requires meditation (see fig. 3) to realize it. Why?

Whereas the foremost concern in Western sports is to respond to an external challenge and to defeat the opponent (or to break an existing record), the foremost concern in kendo is to tame the ego by internalizing challenge. Taming the ego prevents the mind from being swayed by external distractions, enables the practitioner to develop concentration and alertness, and provides the reflexive mechanism necessary to develop kendo skills. But more important than that is to enable its practitioners to channel that discipline to realize personal growth, an issue that will be discussed in further detail in chapter 5. Thus whereas Western sports emphasize relax-ation—the absence of attention and effort—to control anxiety, kendo emphasizes meditation to tame the ego. Although both are designed to bring about a new mental state, the difference in ap-proach stems from a different cultural orientation. Kendo attempts

---

* The term *mushin* is frequently used as a compound, *muga-mushin. Muga* literally means "no-self" (derived from the Sanskrit *anatman*) and *mushin,* "no-mind" (de-rived from the Sanskrit *acitta*). What is negated is the empirical body-mind as an independent state of existence. Muga and mushin point to the same thing—the state of egolessness—but from different perspectives. The former refers to the nega-tion of the physical state and the latter to the negation of the mental state. The Buddhist conceives of the physical and mental entities of existence as inseparable. In this work, however, to simplify matters, the term *mushin* will be used to indicate *muga-mushin.*

FIGURE 3. Kendo Meditation

not only to develop a new mental state, but also to cultivate its norm of ethical behavior in the practice of the art itself; it claims that practice and ethical behavior are inseparable because both stem from taming the ego.

Mushin is described by making reference to three situational cases. First, the kendo practitioner engages in a brief meditation before and after practice. But mushin is not realized in a brief moment of meditation. It is realized through strenuous practice involving sweat, bruises, and blisters. It is realized experientially over a long period, not instantly as one accustomed to a fast-food culture might anticipate. Kendo meditation follows the same rationale observed in Zen: the anticipation of instant realization—that is, enlightenment—through meditation is a delusion. The goal of both is to build a new mental configuration experientially.

Second, although one not accustomed to kendo may associate its practice with violence, practice is actually designed to tame the ego. What this means is that the attribute that kendo practice cultivates must be internalized. What is internalized is called "discipline." Granted that there are other nonviolent ways to realize the same state, because of the influence of Buddhism on the development of kendo, Buddhist thought underlies the manner in which kendo attempts to realize discipline. Whether the manner in question represents violence is a relative question that involves a personal judgment of what violence means. Take an example. A Zen master would render a novice a hard blow to awaken the human potential within him. In this case the blow is not an act of violence. It is an act of compassion to awaken mushin within the practitioner. Likewise, the kendo master who renders a hard blow on the student does not consider it an act of violence but an act designed to enable him to realize *mushin*. Malicious intent is involved in violence, but it is absent among Zen and kendo practitioners.

And third, although mushin can be realized through kendo as well as through other human activities, there is a slight difference between what the two attempt to realize. Compare, for example, the mushin required in kendo practice with that required in studying math, science, or a foreign language. Both require concentration and perseverance. But in the former case, these attributes are designed to develop the speed necessary to cope with an opponent. The attribute involved in cultivating mushin in kendo can be implemented in studying math, and so forth, but not the other way around. The implication here, however, is not that all kendo practitioners excel in academic discipline. There are many Western sports that, like kendo, also require concentration and perseverance. This may be the reason that some young athletes who take part in the Olympics go on to and are successful in graduate or professional schools. They have developed the elements necessary to cope with an academic discipline. Just as some Western athletes are capable of implementing the discipline cultivated in sports in their academic work, so too with some kendo practitioners.

In sum, then, to realize mushin, kendo requires meditation, a subject that will be taken up in detail in chapter 2. What is important to note here, however, is the kind of meditation kendo involves. It is not meditation designed to flee from worldly reality, to realize a state of trance, or to enter the realm of nirvana. Kendo meditation is designed to tame the ego and to realize body-mind integration. *Ki-ai* is the verbal evidence of this integration.

Ki-ai and Body-Mind Integration

There is no adequate English translation for *ki-ai*. A Japanese-English dictionary renders the term as "yell, shout, etc., to hypnotize or mesmerize another person with will power." But this is preposterous. Etymologically the term is a compound, *ki* referring to energy and *ai* to integration.

Historically, the term *ki* is of Chinese origin (*ch'i*). In the context of Chinese philosophy, it is conceived of as a source of life, regarded as a material element, and believed to pervade the universe. But *ki*, when used in the compound (*ki* + *ai*), and in particular when used in the limited context of kendo, refers to a verbal outflow of a synergistic force derived through body-mind integration.

It is not clear how ki-ai originated or when it began to be used in swordsmanship. According to a story, it was conceived of and practiced in late seventh-century Japan by the Yamabushi or Shugenja, members of a Shinto-Taoist-Buddhist cult who roamed about the mountains and allegedly acquired supernatural powers. Ki-ai might have been originated by the members of this cult. But the term began to be understood in a rational context after the founding of Shingon Mikkyo Buddhism in the ninth century.

In classical kendo, the basic forms of ki-ai are *ya* (pronounced "yah") and *to* (pronounced "toh"). Ki-ai that announce the intended targets (e.g., men, kote, do, and tsuki) are also used. The latter verbal forms were formulated after the protective gear was popularized in the eighteenth century and provided referees with a basis for judgment in a match. They are the popular ki-ai observed in kendo practice today. But a kendo ki-ai is not simply a shout meant to "startle or mesmerize" the opponent. It is the verbal revelation, demonstration, and evidence of a synergistic force issuing from the body-mind integration that produces the most important element in kendo combat—namely, decisiveness.

Decisiveness was held to be the most significant factor in battlefield combat. When the samurai was confronted by multiple opponents, there was no time to deal exclusively with any single individual. Instead the samurai had to be instantaneously decisive in order to survive. Decisiveness characterizes many forms of Japanese martial arts (e.g., karate, sumo, and judo).

Boxing differs from karate in that boxing requires repeated blows—in karate the first thrust is decisive. Hence boxing matches last many rounds, while a karate match basically consists of just one round. Western wrestling also takes considerable time, while a sumo match is over in a few seconds. A judo match does last longer, but it too is determined by the *waza ari*, the decisive throw. Likewise, in kendo, the practitioner's shinai requires speed and control, which together produce the decisive snap or thrust.* A sword is not a carpenter's saw going over and over the same cut.† A decisive hit of the kind demanded in kendo requires precision, and precision requires a

---

* A kendo novice tends to slam his shinai down on the intended target. In such a case, he is incapable of instantly making the second and third attacks. A snap supported by a ki-ai is much more effective in combat. A snap is produced by wringing the shinai handle with both hands, like wringing a towel, and slamming the right foot on the floor as one leaps, accompanied by a determined ki-ai. Hence, in kendo, a synergistic force derived from body-mind integration rather than physical strength needs to be cultivated.

† Many schools of swordsmanship are called *Itto-ryu*, "one-sword school." Some may conceive of this term as a contrast to *Nito-ryu*, "school of two swords." But the term *itto* refers to a style designed to create a devastating effect with one decisive slash.

synergistic force. But body-mind integration, not ki-ai, brings about this kind of force. Ki-ai is the product of this integration. As such, it is the mind (mushin), not ki-ai, that needs to be nurtured. An effective ki-ai emerges from one's gut. Shouting in a frenzy is not a ki-ai.

Kama-e and Ma-ai: Positions and Spacing

In kendo there are three basic stances, or *kama-e: jodan, chudan,* and *gedan* (upper, middle, and lower levels). Other forms are variations of these basic three. In jodan (fig. 4), the practitioner holds the shinai above his forehead, poised to strike at the opponent's head, wrist, or body. In chudan (fig. 5), the practitioner holds the shinai in the middle position, aimed for a thrust to the opponent's throat, eyes, or chest, while at the same time maintaining enough maneuverability to leap forward to hit the opponent on the head, wrist, or

FIGURE 4. Jodan Position

FIGURE 5. Chudan Position

body, or to receive the attack. In gedan (fig. 6), the practitioner holds the shinai tilted forward and down, making it difficult for the opponent to leap forward but totally exposing his head for an attack.

Jodan is the aggressive kama-e: the practitioner cannot retreat, there is no effective defense—the only real option is to take the offense. Chudan is the standard kama-e: the practitioner can either attack or receive an attack. Gedan is the defensive kama-e:* the practitioner parries the invited attack and, using the opponent's own

---

* In modern kendo, in the gedan kama-e, one usually puts the right foot forward, points the shinai at the opponent's left knee, and keeps the body straight. But in classical kendo, one puts the left foot forward, points the shinai toward the floor, and slightly tilts the body forward. This stance is referred to as *shumoku-no-ashi* and is discouraged in modern kendo because it hinders leaping speed. But in classical kendo, it is one of the acceptable stances because it provides one with stability and hence the force to cut through.

FIGURE 6. Gedan Position

force, strikes the opponent's body, for example, on a rebound. But gedan can also be an aggressive kama-e, thrusting at the throat from underneath the opponent's defense. In all cases, however, the practitioner must be mindful of the following three elements: the speed of the opponent's attack; one's own attack-speed (including the speed with which one can receive an attack, then transform defense to offense instantly); and the proper judgment of the "distance" between oneself and the opponent. The third element needs explanation.

The term *distance* is a rough translation of *ma-ai*, the root of which is *ma*, "space." As such, the term *distance* can be misleading. As a background for understanding the ma-ai concept, two forms of Japanese arts are described.

The term *ma* is used in the tea ceremony in the sense of the term *ma o toru*, literally "space-evaluation." Actually, the term refers to the host's awareness of the relationship between the principal guest and the environment in which the ceremony is observed. Specifically, it refers to furnishing the team room with a picture scroll, a vase of carefully arranged flowers, ceramic ware of excellent make and design, and other accoutrements tastefully chosen and set out to reflect the personality of the principal guest. Items required for the ceremony, such as cups, kettle, and ladle, are strategically placed to minimize the movements that the host must make in executing the prescribed steps of the ceremony. *Ma,* then, is a term that implies the creative utilization of space—that is, the ability to control space.

The art of flower arrangement, like kendo, employs three levels of position. Here high, middle, and low levels represent heaven, human, and earth, the human dimension serving as a bridge between heaven and earth and so giving an overall harmony to the composition. This human dimension is, however, not fixed. After all, each individual has his or her own personality, so that there are no limits to creativity. Ultimately, though, the human dimension must merge with nature, with heaven and earth, to bring about total harmony. Hence, when a master of this art speaks of an overall harmony, he or she is not speaking only about the flower arrangement, but also about the shape of the vase appropriate to the flower design, and the entire context that determines the choice of vase and design (e.g., the size and style of the alcove in which the flower arrangement is to be placed, the size and style of the room, and the nature of the occasion for the display). The art of flower arrangement too requires the creative utilization of space and the ability to control it, although the term *ma* is not employed.

Ma, however, is not uniquely Japanese. In modern ballet, for example, an accomplished ballerina has total control of space. She has the ability to project the movements of the dance from a perspective that displays perfect harmony and elegant style. It is this overall pattern of movement that elicits the undivided attention of the audience.

In kendo, ma-ai generally refers to the distance between the tips of the opponents' shinai when both are in chudan position. Theoretically, the shinai should cross each other about two or three inches below their tips. However, this basic definition cannot be applied if the opponent takes a jodan or gedan stance, or a variation of the basic forms. For example, the *wakigama-e* (fig. 7), in which the shinai is held in gedan but to the rear, concealing the shinai tip; or the *hasso* (fig. 8), in which the shinai is held in jodan but to the side, like a baseball bat. In these cases the opponent cannot judge the distance by the shinai tips and so must take into account the opponent's degree of alertness and speed as well as the moment and the angle of charge. And, of course, when a practitioner faces multiple opponents, the general definition of ma-ai, "distance," would hardly have any meaning at all. Ma-ai, then, involves more than just the judgment of distance between opponents.

FIGURE 7. Wakigama-e Position

FIGURE 8. Hasso Position

Ma-ai actually refers to space. Like a ballet dancer, a kendo practitioner needs to control space—to develop the ability to size up the situation in which he finds himself and to place himself in a strategically advantageous position.

But although ma-ai literally refers to spacing, it is also associated with the ability to read the time—a fraction of a second—it will take for the practitioner to leap forward before the opponent's charge. The ma-ai between two experienced kendo practitioners is, therefore, frequently stretched out in order to accommodate the unexpected. This brings us back to the term *kama-e*, previously defined as stance.

Kama-e indicates the degree of control the practitioner has over space and time. As such, kama-e and ma-ai are correlated: an effective kama-e reveals an effective ma-ai control. Interestingly, though, because kama-e requires the proper reading of ma-ai, many skilled swordsmen in the past spoke of the kama-e of no-kama-e. To those men, kama-e did not involve the manner in which one holds the sword. It was a mental attitude. Hence, Yagyu Sekishusai, also know as Sekishu, (1529–1606) emphasized the importance of *Muto-ryu* (the school of no-sword).* To him, the sword existed only in the mind. And Hayashizaki Chosuke (seventeenth century), who contributed much in developing *i-ai* (tentatively translated as "quick-draw skill"; see p. 24 for details) spoke of conquering the opponent while the sword remains in the sheath.

To be sure, kama-e, to a large extent, is a state of mind, but to master the art of the kama-e of no-kama-e first requires the mastery of kama-e, which involves the proper reading of ma-ai. Muto-ryu and i-ai also require mastery of ma-ai. It is dangerous for a novice to use the kama-e of no-kama-e or to engage in Muto-ryu or i-ai in actual combat.

Kama-e, then, refers to a stance. But because kama-e requires the proper reading of ma-ai (the ability to control space) and also because ma-ai constantly changes according to the opponent's movement, kama-e actually is more than a stylized stance. It requires direct cognitive ability. In this context, then, kama-e involves a mental attitude—alertness of a kind derived through intense concentration. This mental attribute contributed to the development of the kama-e of no-kama-e, Muto-ryu, and i-ai.

Suki and Zanshin: Openings and Alertness

An effective kama-e (either kama-e itself or the kama-e of no-kama-e) leaves no opening for the opponent to attack. In the kendo

---

* Chujo-ryu (also called Tomita-ryu or Toda-ryu), founded by Toda Seigen (sixteenth century) in present-day Fukui Prefecture, also referred to his school as Muto-ryu. Seigen first trained himself in short-sword fighting, which requires the instant reading of the opponent's intent, as well as ma-ai, and charging in at the moment before the opponent's attack. He later became partially blind but still managed to defend himself. Perhaps it was his blindness that enabled him to read the oppo-

lexicon, an opening is referred to as *suki*. A kendo practitioner with no suki projects an intimidating kama-e. The term, however, has another meaning. There is no suki in an accomplished ballet dancer, that is, no futile, wasteful, or meaningless movement. It is the same with an accomplished kendo practitioner. Each movement, no matter how minute, is distinct and has meaning to the practitioner's overall strategy.

A perfect kama-e leaves no suki, and a kama-e without suki is evidence that the practitioner is capable of combat without futile movements. The practitioner's potential for subsequent movements is therefore epitomized in his kama-e, a kama-e without suki, just as the ballerina's potential for subsequent movements is epitomized in her opening stance, a stance without futile movements. But an effective kama-e of a kendo practitioner (or a perfect opening stance of a ballerina) represents the crystallization of consummate effort over the course of years, during which the practitioner coped with the issue of ma-ai through intense combat practice.

Although the practitioner may have perfected a kama-e through years of combat practice, there is always the chance that he or she may miss a target. What position should the practitioner then take? Here the issue of *zanshin*, sustained alertness, needs to be taken up. Two examples are presented below:

In the first case, the attacker attacks and misses a target. The receiver of the attack would have the advantage. He would be in a position to calmly observe the attacker's opening. So after the attack, the attacker must get away from the receiver's range of attack, turn quickly, and transform defense into offense instantly. In the second case, although the attacker had missed the first target, normally he would be able to see a second opening in the receiver's defense but would not be able to carry through the second attack.

---

nent's intent intuitively without being distracted. Yamaoka Tesshu (1836–88), whom we will discuss in chapter 3, also identified his school as Muto-ryu. Swordsmen, who have developed considerable skill, seem to have preferred Muto-ryu.

These two examples provide the necessary grounds to examine zanshin, sustained alertness. Inherent in this concept is a determined attitude never to "abandon ship" (never leave an opening and constantly seek the opponent's openings) and to instantly launch a second or third attack by transforming defense into offense. The term *instantly* is crucial because zanshin requires alertness—even after the completion of an attack—of a kind that would enable the attacker to cope with an unexpected situation in a split second. What position should a practitioner take if the initial attack succeeds? He should still maintain zanshin. In actual combat, a samurai was trained to be ready to launch a sutemi attack (see p. 3) with the last drop of his energy even if seriously wounded. Moreover, even if the first attack dealt a mortal blow, the samurai assumed that he was surrounded by other opponents on all four sides.

Zanshin, then, is sustained alertness with the aim of assuring strategic victory. It is also an attitude that applies to work: complete a task beyond what is expected, and expect the unexpected.

Sutemi and Heijo-Shin: "Go-for-Broke" Attack and Mental Calm

The term *sutemi,* used previously, now needs elaboration. Sutemi is an attack based on desperation when, for example, the practitioner encounters a superior opponent—an opponent with an intimidating kama-e. In such a case, a novice would find that sutemi is the only effective form of attack. Nevertheless, because it is born of desperation, this kind of attack is rarely employed by a skilled practitioner. A skilled practitioner is expected to maintain mental calm at all times. Mental calm, in this case, is called *heijo-shin* (literally, mental "evenness," the absence of emotional swings).* One without emotional

---

* Both sutemi and heijo-shin emerge from mushin in that the absence of intrusion of intellect characterizes both. What differentiates the two is the psychological basis from which mushin is derived: sutemi is derived from desperation, heijo-shin from calmness. Heijo-shin was initially conceived in T'ang China, where it was referred to as *ping-ch'ang hsin.* There is no Buddhist Sanskrit equivalent of this term.

swings is in control of himself. As such, that person is capable of reading the intent of his opponent—the opponent's potential movement and the moment of his attack.

Heijo-shin produces what is referred to as *go-no-sen*, landing a hit by allowing the opponent to attack first, leaving only a fraction of an inch between the opponent's sword and the practitioner's own body. The expression "leaving only a fraction of an inch" is significant. Although heijo-shin connotes the absence of emotional swings, it also requires the absence of fear, doubt, and hesitation. Absence of fear enables the practitioner to move according to his will. Absence of doubt enables the practitioner to face the opponent with confidence. And absence of hesitation enables the practitioner to render a decisive hit. These skills cannot be developed without heijo-shin. Go-no-sen, derived from heijo-shin, however, is a skill cultivated only through years of training in ma-ai spacing, which is mastered only after grueling practice.

But *go-no-sen* is a classical kendo term to indicate a counterblow. Modern kendo refers to the same as *debana*, landing a hit just as the opponent attacks. But there is a distinct difference between go-no-sen and debana. In the former, heijo-shin is strongly emphasized; in the latter, timing is emphasized. Modern kendo is concerned with the particular (timing), classical kendo with the general (intuitive response associated with overall strategy). Regardless of the manner in which heijo-shin is interpreted, it refers to a state of mind acquired through years of sutemi practice.

Dojo: The Hall of Discipline

The kendo hall of practice is called a *dojo*. It is a sacred site and should be kept clean. Usually a Shinto deity is enshrined in a dojo as a symbolic representation of purity, that is, of the "pure" mind or mushin. (Although deities are characteristic of Shinto and mushin is a Buddhist concept, Shinto-Buddhist syncretism characterizes Japanese religion.)[4] Because *dojo* is an important term in Japanese martial arts, the term's etymological origin and the manner in which it has been assimilated into a Sino-Japanese vocabulary need to be described.

The term *dojo* is derived from the Buddhist Sanskrit *bodhimanda,* meaning the "site of enlightenment." But when the term was rendered into Sino-Japanese characters (*dojo*), it took on a different nuance of meaning. *Do* (pronounced "doh") means "the way of life," and *jo* means "the site." *Dojo* refers to the site to cultivate the way of life. The term *do* therefore is used in a variety of art forms—for example, *budo,* the way of life of those who practice martial arts; *sado,* the way of life of those who practice tea ceremony; *kado,* the way of life of those who practice flower arrangement. Kendo (*ken* + *do*), therefore, does not refer only to developing swordsman's skills; it refers to the way of life of those who cultivate those skills. Considering the etymological origin of the term *dojo,* the Buddhist impact on kendo is distinct.

In spite of the great impact Buddhist thought has had on swordsmanship, many kendo schools were founded at Shinto shrines. One of the greatest medieval swordsmen, Iizasa Choisai (c. 1387–1488), is said to have developed his skills under the inspiration of the Katori Shinto deity. Interestingly, though, it is also said that Miyamoto Musashi (1584–1645), on his way to battle a crowd of opponents, passed by a Shinto shrine and was tempted to pray for his victory, but did not, saying, "Gods and buddhas should be honored and respected, not depended upon." This practice continues today as novices are taught to honor and respect a Shinto deity enshrined in the dojo, but not to depend on it. More will be said about these two skilled swordsmen later.

Because the dojo is the hall of discipline, the kendo practitioner bows as he or she enters it. There should be no small talk among the practitioners and no bombastic commands from the instructor inside the dojo. Some skilled classical kendo instructors therefore did not teach in words, but only through body-to-body crushing combat practice.

Because the purpose of kendo is to realize mushin, the kendo practitioner bows to his opponent before and after practice and takes a position known as *sonkyo*, stooping down with knees bent (fig. 9). This demonstrates the highest respect to the opponent, because the opponent is the means through which the practitioner realizes the true self—just as a Zen monk pays homage to the Dharma, the truth, through which he comes to realize the true self.

The popularity of Zen, however, has contributed to a trend of making Zen formalized, ritualized, and commercialized. In kendo there is no such empty practice. True, the kendo practitioner may find it difficult to enter the dojo and put on the bogu; he may face a

FIGURE 9. Sonkyo Position

slump, and ask why he has to push himself to such strenuous practice. But those who survive these attacks of slacking motivation know that neglect of practice leads only to despair. So the practitioner makes the efforts, pushes himself, enters the dojo, puts on the bogu, faces the opponent, attacks and is attacked, and suffers bruises. The practitioner looks straight into the opponent's eyes; sweat stings his own eyes, pours down the face. Nonetheless, the practitioner knows that he or she cannot retreat, for retreat invites an attack. In this state of exhaustion, the practitioner develops one-pointed concentration, attacks, and hits the target. There is a moment of silence, then a sense of physical accomplishment. Physical accomplishment produces self-fulfillment, and self-fulfillment produces self-confidence. The practitioner has conquered himself/herself, and then reverently takes the sonkyo position.

There is no hypocrisy when the practitioner faces an opponent and looks straight into the opponent's eyes; for at that moment one is in fact looking to one's own self. Perspiration has washed away the superficial mask one wears to walk through life. It is this self—the ego-suppressed self, the naked self, the true self—what was referred to as mushin—with which the practitioner had confronted the opponent.

The kendo practitioner who has experienced this kind of practice tilts his head—a sign of respect to the hall of discipline—as he leaves that hall. Arrogance and pompousness are absent in a true practitioner. Humility and respect are the marks of a true practitioner. The practitioners who reveal these attributes are called those who abide in the way of the sword, *ken* + *do*, in every walk of life.

2
The Impact of Buddhist Thought on the Development of Swordsmanship

IN THE PREVIOUS CHAPTER, the Buddhist impact on kendo was described in general terms. In this chapter its impact on the formulation of two schools of classical kendo is described.

The impacts of Shingon Mikkyo on Katori-ryu and of Zen on Yagyu-ryu are distinct. In describing these impacts, however, different approaches need to be observed. In the case of Katori-ryu, although its historical lineage—the founder's life, his devotion to Shingon Mikkyo, and his skills—has been documented, neither its founder nor his followers left texts that recount the impact of Shingon Mikkyo on the development of this school. Fortunately, however, the Katori-ryu tradition has been kept alive. The description of this school is, therefore, my own interpretation based on observation. In the case of the Yagyu-ryu, texts that describe the Zen impact on that school are available. The description of this school is based on my interpretation of these texts.

Shingon Mikkyo's Influence on the Katori-ryu

HISTORICAL BACKGROUND

The Katori-Kashima area, located about fifty miles northeast from central Tokyo and renowned as the sites of the Katori and Kashima

Shinto Shrines, is the origin of the Japanese martial arts tradition.[5]
It is alleged that these shrines were established in the prehistorical
period. The deities of these shrines—Futsunushi-no-kami and
Takemikazu-chi-no-kami, respectively—have traditionally been
worshipped by many eminent swordsmen, such as Iizasa Choisai
and Tsukahara Bokuden, who originated from this area. Many
medieval swordsmen made pilgrimages to these shrines. Even today,
kendo dojo in Japan enshrine either or both of these deities.

The Katori-ryu was systematized by Iizasa Choisai (1387–1488).[6]
Active in the early Warring States period, he initially served the
Chibas, the local lords of the present Chiba Prefecture. But after
the defeat of the Chibas, he retreated to Umekiyama near the Katori Shrine and trained students. Choisai was an accomplished
master in the use of the sword (long and short), lance (*yari*), halberd (*naginata*), staffs (*bo* and *jo*), and quick-draw skill (i-ai). He
worshipped the Katori Shinto deity, and was a Shingon Mikkyo
Buddhist practitioner. Shingon Mikkyo was the agent of Shinto-
Buddhist syncretism.[7]

The ancient tradition of Katori-ryu allegedly has been transmitted
without change since Choisai's day. Currently, its tradition is transmitted by Iizasa Yasutada (representing the twentieth generation removed from Choisai), whose dojo, reconstructed some 250 years ago
and still in use, is located in the suburb of Sahara City (near the
present Narita International Airport), at a site not far from where
Choisai first established his dojo. The head instructor of this school
is Otake Risuke, a man in his late seventies and a faithful practitioner
of Shingon Mikkyo. Otake's dojo (called the Jinbukan) is located a
few miles away from the Iizasa dojo. Otake is unpretentious, and his
students, both male and female, reflect the gentility of his character
and the depth of his discipline.

Katori-ryu does not employ shinai as does kendo. Instead, it uses
bokuto (referred to as *bokken* according to this school), a hard
wooden sword carved from oak or loguate wood, which is capable of

breaking bones and inflicting bruises and can be lethal. There are two kinds of bokken—the long form, which is less than three feet long, and the short form, which is less than two feet. This school also trains students in the use of bo and jo, yari, and naginata (all made of hardwood), and the practice of i-ai. Students faithfully follow the medieval samurai tradition of engaging in a variety of martial arts practices. Further, they do not use bogu, as do kendo students.* Instead, they observe *kumitachi*, prearranged combat practice, which developed out of and was designed for actual battlefield combat, rather than out of dojo practice. Thus, Katori-ryu's kumitachi is different from kendo's *kata* (prearranged stylized form) practice. Whereas the latter is practiced in ten fragmented steps and is ritualistically performed by masters at times of exhibitions, or by students preparing for rank promotion, the former consists of consistent flow characterized by speed of movement, dynamic execution, and realistic character. Speed of movement cultivates good reflexes; dynamic execution stabilizes the body; and realistic character cultivates mental alertness.

This kind of practice is also observed in i-ai. Although the term is commonly translated as "quick-draw skill," it is not limited to this. I-ai is a skill developed in combating opponents within a limited space, where the movement of a weapon is limited by physical obstacles; in darkness, where one must rely only on instinct; and in countering surprise attacks, when alertness of a high order is required. Accordingly, i-ai requires the development of the skills to handle a weapon effectively and maneuver the body with ease within a limited space. These skills include slashing by a twist of the wrist, thrusting by rapidly drilling in and out within a few inches of space, and, above all, having sharp instincts and keen alertness.

---

* Because of its refusal to equip practitioners with bogu and shinai, Katori-ryu has isolated itself in its birthplace.

Shingon Mikkyo's impact on Katori-ryu requires an understanding of three doctrinal issues: emptiness (*sunyata*), the source of a "secret" energy (*adhisthana*); *bodhicitta*, the agent of integration through which this kind of energy is derived; and *sanmitsu* practices, which verify that integration.

EMPTINESS: THE SOURCE OF "SECRET" ENERGY

Emptiness does not mean nothingness or void. It means that phenomena are absent of an essence; that is, they are neither absolute nor sovereign. Take, for example, the case of oxygen and hydrogen atoms. They are absent of an essence, so they combine, change, and produce water. Emptiness is, therefore, the source of phenomenal change. However, whereas emptiness is taken as an "ontological" concept* in the Indian tradition, it is taken as an experiential concept in the Sino-Japanese tradition (emptying, *k'o-k'ung* in Chinese and *kuzuru* in Japanese). A Zen parable to illustrate the experiential aspect of emptiness is presented below:

Once a young man trained in Western philosophy visited a monk, with the intent to engage in a debate. The monk led the young man to his guest room and offered him a cup of tea. The young man, ignoring the cup of tea, immediately began to engage in a long discourse. After a while, the monk poured some more tea into his guest's cup. The young man shouted, "It's spilling!" He went to the window to get rid of the old tea. The monk then shouted, "While you're getting rid of the old tea, get rid of old ideas too so you can receive fresh ones."

Emptiness in the Sino-Japanese tradition is conceived in a verbal context, that is, emptying fixed and frozen concepts in order to

---

* The emptiness concept is derived from the Indian *prajna* (wisdom) school and was systematized by Nagarjuna (second century CE). The term *ontology* used here refers to this emptiness doctrine. But because this doctrine negates phenomenal existence as ultimate reality, the term is used in a very loose sense.

develop new horizons of thought. In this context, emptiness is conceived of as a creative force. To illustrate this version of emptiness, we now refer to Kukai.

Kukai (774–835), literally meaning Ocean of Emptiness, is the Japanese systematizer of Shingon Mikkyo. He described emptiness in the following manner:

> The Great Space [emptiness], boundless and silent,
>   encompasses ten thousand images [phenomena] within its
>   vital force;
> The Great Ocean [emptiness], deep and still, embraces ten
>   thousand elements in a single drop;
> The all-embracing [Mahavairocana] is the mother of all things.[8]

Shingon Mikkyo personifies emptiness as Dharmakaya Mahavairocana. Literally, *dharmakaya* (*hosshin*) means the "truth-body," the "body of emptiness." In the Shingon Mikkyo context, it symbolizes the creative force of the cosmos. Mahavairocana therefore is referred to as the "Great Light" (*Dainichi*), with the power to create, nurture, regulate, and encompass all things.[9]

The ultimate aim of Shingon Mikkyo is to enable its practitioner to realize integration with Dharmakaya Mahavairocana. Integration is technically referred to as *sokushin-jobutsu*, or "human-Buddha integration."[10] But here the term *Buddha*, of course, does not refer to the historical Buddha. It refers to the Mahavairocana cosmos.

Shingon Mikkyo's integration theory bears distinct similarity with Spinoza's "god is nature" (*deus sive natura*) concept. It is also similar to the modern ecological concept, which asserts that humankind is a part of the natural environment, that all elements within it are subject to change, and that this change takes place within an organic unit characterized by harmony. Of course, ecology is a biological theory, whereas Shingon Mikkyo is a soteriological theory. The question that arises in the context of Shingon Mikkyo is what makes integration possible.

BODHICITTA: THE AGENT OF INTEGRATION

Bodhicitta literally means "enlightened mind," but here it refers to the wisdom inherent in all human beings, which enables them to realize integration[11] with the Mahavairocana cosmos and thereby makes it possible for them to acquire a force beyond that limited by the empirical self by eliminating the ego-clouded vision. The *Mahavairocana-sutra*, one of the major textual sources of Shingon Mikkyo, therefore, defines *bodhicitta* as the true self.[12] To this extent, *bodhicitta* and mushin are similar. But two questions arise: Since this integration theory claims that something is inherent in the makeup of sentient being, is not *bodhicitta* an essentialist doctrine? And if mushin and *bodhicitta* are similar, why use two different terms?

First, the idea that *bodhicitta* is inherent in human beings is an essentialist view. As such, it goes contrary to the Buddhist concept of emptiness. But *bodhicitta* is a metaphor, a figure of speech or a means, just like numerals are means to understand mathematical truth but are not that truth.

Second, the terms *mushin* and *bodhicitta* do not refer to different states of mind, but describe the same state—the true self—from different perspectives.* *Mushin* is a psychological term referring to

---

* The term *mushin*, rather than *bodhicitta*, was popularly used in classical kendo because of a historical circumstance: the emergence of the Shinkage-ryu systematized by Kozumi Ise-no-kami (1508–77), advanced by Yagyu Sekishu, and, in the early seventeenth century, popularized in Edo (present-day Tokyo) by Yagyu Munenori (1571–1646). This school was then designated as the Yagyu Shinkage-ryu. Munenori popularized the Yagyu school by synthesizing Zen and classical kendo under the instruction of Takuan, a Zen monk and his spiritual mentor. (The Yagyu-ryu, Munenori, and Takuan will be dealt with in detail later.) *Mushin*, although not a term unique to Zen, is nevertheless extensively used in Zen. Many medieval samurai were both Shingon Mikkyo and Zen practitioners because of the close doctrinal affinity between them.

that which enables one to realize body-mind integration. *Bodhicitta*
is a soteriological term that involves the unconditional acceptance
of the proposition that the wisdom to realize integration is inherent
in all human beings. But in their function and application, they are
identical. They are realized through taming (if not total destruction
of) the ego, which in turn enables one to realize a synergistic force.
Thus, it will be recalled that *mushin*, primarily a Zen term, is frequently described as *muga-mushin* (see footnote, p. 4), the negation
of the empirical body and mind that brings about the true state of
being. Shingon Mikkyo posits a similar notion, body-mind integration, the realm in which the empirical body and mind are integrated
with the Mahavairocana cosmos.

Because Shingon Mikkyo presupposes that *bodhicitta* is inherent,
it emphasizes practice to verify that inherent quality. Practice specifically refers to sanmitsu practice.

SANMITSU PRACTICE: EVIDENCE OF INTEGRATION

Sanmitsu refers to three types of practice—physical, vocal, and
mental.

Physical integration is verified by a *mudra* (a stylized finger gesture). The practitioner places the right palm over the left palm, with
the right and left thumbs touching and forming an oval shape with
the palms.

This is the sign of physical integration (human-cosmos integration) and is referred to as *hokkai-jo-in* (*dharmadhatu-samadhi-
mudra*). The five left fingers symbolize the five elements of humankind, and the five right fingers the five elements of the cosmos.* A
mudra, like a dance, is a physical expression of one's inner feeling.

Vocal integration is verified through a *mantra*. A mantra is an old

---

* The five elements are earth, water, fire, wind, and space. Attempts to describe
the world in terms of its component elements is not peculiar to Shingon Mikkyo.
Both Western and Eastern philosophers have explained the constitution of the

Indian custom found in the Vedic literature. There, a mantra is a chant used to praise the gods. But Shingon Mikkyo conceives of it as a verbal truth formula, evidencing the perfection of integration verbally.

Mental integration is verified through *yogic* meditation. *Yoke*, meaning "to join," is cognate with *yoga*. Yoga requires concentration, just as does sexual union, and it is equally exhausting and fulfilling. The parallel does not imply that sexual union and yoga are psychologically identical. But they are similar, inasmuch as both represent union, ecstasy, and procreation. However, whereas sex represents a basic human instinct designed by evolution to create a new body, yoga is a discipline designed to create a new mental configuration, human-cosmos integration.

In sum, sanmitsu signals—through the media of body, voice, and mind—that the practitioner has realized integration with the Mahavairocana cosmos.

The Katori-ryu observes the sanmitsu practices. It uses:

(a) the mudra finger gesture;
(b) the mantra verbal formula, which is referred to as *ki-ai*; and
(c) meditation, which is referred to as *mokuso*.

---

world in terms of its elements. For example, Empedocles spoke of four elements, while the Pythagoreans and Aristotelians, as well as Indian philosophical schools (Upanisad, Samkhya, and Vaisesika), spoke of five. These philosophers and philosophical schools, however, took elements to be forms of matter with distinct physical properties. But Shingon Mikkyo's five elements symbolize the five aspects of reality—the body of "emptiness" that is conceived of as a creative force. Thus earth symbolizes the creative force as such; water, that this creative force flows to all corners of the universe; fire, that it burns up errors; wind, that it moves freely; and space, that it encompasses all things. Actually, Shingon Mikkyo speaks of six elements:[13] the five elements of the cosmos, symbolizing the creative force, and a sixth symbolizing the human consciousness upon which the first five elements are reflected. Technically, the first five elements represent Shingon Mikkyo's "ontological" doctrine and the sixth its epistemological doctrine.

Because the Katori-ryu is the first systematized form of Japanese martial arts, its sanmitsu practice is faithfully observed in present-day kendo, as well as in other forms of Japanese martial arts in order to realize body-mind integration.[14]

Many medieval swordsmen were attracted to Shingon Mikkyo, because this school asserts that a synergistic force gushes out from human-cosmos integration. Many of them were therefore mystics. But although Shingon Mikkyo's integration may be understood theoretically, it is difficult to ascertain empirically. In swordsmanship, a popular culture, however, it can be ascertained: without integration, its practitioner cannot engage in a practice characterized by speed of movement and dynamic execution, and cannot experience the synergistic force that gushes out of it. Many swordsmen believed in a synergistic force—derived from the integration of human beings with a superior power—because their survival was at stake. In the case of Iizasa Choisai, however, it provided more than belief in a superior power.

Although he was reared in the Warring States period and was exposed to actual battlefield combat experience, after the defeat of the Chibas, he retreated to Umekiyama. It is here, during the time of his retreat, that he conceived of the expression *"heiho* is *heiho,"*[15] a pun. The term *heiho* has two meanings, pronounced the same but written in different characters. The first refers to martial arts (兵法), the second to peace (平法). The expression, therefore, means "the way of martial arts is the way to peace." Although this may sound paradoxical, what the expression actually means is that the discipline involved in the development of martial arts (heretofore cited as the cultivation of mushin and here cited as bodhicitta) is applicable to the arts of peace. Choisai, a devoted Shingon Mikkyo believer, apparently understood the ultimate purpose of that school's practice. Thus he refused to engage in duels. On one occasion, when he was forced to, it is said that he demonstrated that synergistic force by levitating himself. The astonished challenger meekly left. Choisai, like many medieval ninja, apparently was a skillful hypnotist as well.

Zen's Influence on the Yagyu-Ryu

THE ZEN MASTER TAKUAN

Known in full as Takuan Soho (1573–1645), Takuan[16] was affiliated with Rinzai Zen. Sixteenth-century Japan was the period of Warring States. The Tokugawas unified Japan in the early seventeenth century. Through the synthesis of Zen and swordsmanship, Takuan helped Yagyu Munenori (1571–1646) transmute classical kendo from a combat skill to a discipline for restraining battle-hardened samurai during the peaceful Tokugawa period (1603–1868). This contributed to maintaining law and order and won the Yagyu-ryu the official sanction of the Tokugawas.

Takuan was born to the family of Akiba Tsunanori, a samurai in the service of Yamana Sozen, a *daimyo* (provincial lord) in the province of Tajima in north-central Japan. As a child he entered Shonen-ji, a Pure Land temple, and then at fourteen the Zen monastery of Sokyo-ji, where he was initiated into Zen discipline by Kisen. When he was nineteen Kisen died, and Takuan continued his studies under Toho. Later, Takuan followed Toho to Kyoto and spent seven years studying under Soen, a renowned Zen master of the time. Subsequently, he went to Sakai, a teeming port city near Osaka, where he studied arts and literature under the instruction of Bensei, while continuing to engage in Zen meditation practice under Kokyo, a representative in Sakai of the Daioku-ji Zen tradition. He received his Zen certification at the age of thirty-two. Takuan's life as an itinerant monk was characterized by discipline, poverty, and hard work. It is said that when he washed his clothes, he had to remain naked until they dried because he had only one set.

In 1605, Kokyo died. The following year Takuan became the head monk of Nanshu-ji monastery in Kyoto; and in 1609, by imperial decree, he was promoted to head monk of Daitoku-ji, one of the most prestigious Zen monasteries in Kyoto. Daitoku-ji had had the warm support of emperors such as Hanazono (r. 1308–18) and Go-daigo (r. 1318–39) in the past and was traditionally recognized as an imperially sponsored monastery.

The Tokugawas, intending to establish a system of feudal rule with themselves in firm control, took steps to subdue the immensely wealthy and influential Buddhist monasteries. As the head of Dai-toku-ji, Takuan resisted. In 1629, he was accused of treason, removed from office, and sent into exile. It was Yagyu Munenori who was instrumental in obtaining his pardon and inviting him to Edo, the Tokugawa capital. He was warmly received by the third shogun, Ie-mitsu, in 1632. For more than ten years thereafter he lived at Tokai-ji, a monastery built by Iemitsu not far from the shogun's castle. Takuan frequently visited Iemitsu and eventually became his spiritual mentor.

At this point, neither the Tokugawas, having succeeded in gaining complete control of Japan, nor Takuan, having observed the radical change in the political climate, considered the Daitoku-ji incident a major issue. Daitoku-ji subsequently regained its independence, remaining an imperially sponsored monastery free from the control of the shogunate. But Takuan resigned as head monk of Daitoku-ji and devoted himself to writing.

Two of his works, which deal with the samurai, are the *Fudo-chi Shinmyo Roku*[17] and the *Tai-A Ki*.[18] The first focuses on perfecting the mind in order to perfect swordsmanship. The second focuses on perfecting the mind in order to perfect the samurai character. A summary of these two texts* is presented below.

---

* In presenting a summary of these two texts, I have referred to the original, not the translated version. The texts are contained in the *Takuan osho zenshu* (Tokyo: Takuan osho zenshu kanko-kai, 1928). But here I am not summarizing the contents

FUDO-CHI SHINMYO ROKU: THE DEVELOPMENT OF SWORDSMAN SKILL

Fudo (Acala) is a Buddhist deity symbolizing immovability, and *chi* (*prajna*) means wisdom, insight into emptiness. *Fudo-chi* therefore refers to a wisdom that is not moved by externals. It corresponds to mushin. *Shinmyo* (*saddharma*) refers to a synergistic force issuing from body-mind integration. As such, *shinmyo* is a term that describes the functional aspect of mushin. *Roku* means a manual. This text is a manual describing how a synergistic force can best be applied in swordsmanship. Thus, although the central theme of this text is emptiness, it is not an ontological–epistemological insight; it is the implementation of this synergistic force. The contents are described in five thematic categories.

The first theme is delusion. Delusion is a state of mind attached to the attacker. A samurai in this state is deprived of freedom of movement because delusion (attachment) prevents the attainment of a flow-state.

The second theme is immovable wisdom (fudo-chi). Fudo is a Buddhist deity who symbolizes the destruction of delusion: his eyes are fierce to penetrate delusion; he holds a sword in his right hand, a rope in his left to cut off and bind delusion; and fire burns at his back to burn delusion. The text, therefore, says that without fudo-chi, the samurai would not be able to deal with multiple opponents, for if he were attached to one opponent, he would leave himself open for attack by others. Paradoxical though it may sound, the "immovable" gives rise to the "movable," for only the mind unmoved by externals is capable of producing reflexive action, an action which the text refers to as "without a hairbreadth between [actions]."

The third theme is freedom of movement. If the samurai's mind

---

item by item as they appear in the texts. I have instead rearranged and thematically contextualized them to enable a better understanding of the texts' major themes.

were focused on the opponent's bodily movement, it would become attached to that movement; if it were focused on the opponent's sword, it would be attached to that sword; and if it were focused on slashing the opponent, it would become attached to his own sword. None of these states would produce reflexive action. Thus the mind should not be focused singly on anything. This does not mean that mental function should cease—for if it did, the opponent would seize that moment and attack. One should therefore make the entire body the mind, that is, integrate body and mind, which the fourth theme defines as *honshin*.

The fourth theme deals with the "original state of mind" (*honshin*) and the "deluded mind" (*moshin*). Honshin is the true self; moshin is the empirical self. The former is free from attachment to externals and produces the flow-state. The latter is attached to externals and prevents the flow-state.

The fifth theme is the "mind of no-abiding." Terms such as *wisdom, indestructible mind, nonattachment, mushin*, are synonyms. They all refer to the "mind of no-abiding" and characterize honshin. The state of no-abiding can best be described through examples. When we walk, our mind does not "abide" (rest, stop, etc.) on our legs. If it did, it would hinder the freedom of our stride. When we are hard at work with our hands, our mind does not "abide" on our hands. If it did, it would hinder the freedom of their movement. The mind that is free from abiding on a fixed point produces a flow-state which the text refers to as "perfect freedom." Thus the text states that the samurai's mind should neither abide on the opponent nor on the opponent's sword; neither should it abide in the desire to crush the opponent nor the fear of being crushed.

TAI-A KI: THE DEVELOPMENT OF SAMURAI CHARACTER

Tai-A refers to a legendary sword of unsurpassed quality, capable of cutting through steel and of withstanding any assault. The character of the samurai should be likewise—of unsurpassed quality. *Ki* means an essay. This text is an instructional manual on the development of samurai character during peacetime. Again, the contents of the text are described in five thematic categories.

The first theme is "Triumph without Being Moved." Takuan claims that the ultimate goal of swordsmanship is not simply to master sword skills or to develop physical prowess, but to create the human character unmoved by external distractions.

The second theme is "Triumph without a Sword." Here Takuan recounts a Zen tale: A samurai dedicated to perfecting his skill as a swordsman once approached a fragile Zen monk by the roadside and asked him for instructions. The monk stood silently for a moment, then he picked up a fallen twig and drew a circle on the ground. The samurai simply stared at the circle in utter confusion. Suddenly the monk attacked, throwing the samurai to the ground and hitting him with all his strength. The samurai absorbed the blows, knelt before the monk, then thanked him and walked away. The circle represents harmony, taking the edges off the samurai's character, which stick out like a drawn sword ready for combat. What the monk conveyed by the circle was the need for the samurai to develop a rounded (mellow), not pompous, character. It is this kind of character that contributes to sustaining peace among all people.

The third theme is "Triumph without Injury." If he is challenged, a disciplined samurai would still respect the dignity of his opponent: he would draw his sword but would not deal a fatal blow. Instead, he would handle the opponent with ease so that the opponent realizes for himself the futility of his effort. This theme forms the basis of Yagyu-ryu's *katsujin-ken*, life-rendering-sword (see p. 37).

The fourth theme is "Triumph in Silence." What happens if two swordsmen, each with an irresistible Tai-A sword, meet face to face? Here Takuan cites a passage that many Zen tracts refer to—the story of the "silence of the Buddha." As the story goes, Buddha Sakyamuni was about to deliver a sermon at Mount Grdhrakuta, but instead he simply held up a flower. The congregation remained confused. Only

Kasyapamatanga smiled. The Zen notion of the "transmission of the Dharma without words" is derived from this story. The essence of the story is that words are not necessary for those who share the same spiritual experience. Hence, the two samurai with the Tai-A swords, having shared the same experience, would smile and part, completely understanding each other. Skilled swordsmen, therefore, need not engage in a duel. By looking at each other, they would be able to evaluate each other's skill and character.

The fifth theme is "Insight." In swordsmanship, as in Zen, insight is valued above intellectual apprehension. For example, the samurai should not focus on a particular point, such as the tip of the sword. If he does, he would become attached to that tip and would not be able to attack with lightning speed. To realize lightning speed requires instantaneous perception of the opponent's total body-mind movement. Perception of particulars is derived through the intellect, while perception of totality is derived through insight. A cultured samurai should be able to perceive an event that he confronts from a larger social perspective.

The central theme running through both of Takuan's texts, then, is mushin. In the *Fudo-chi Shinmyo Roku*, mushin enables a swordsman to develop skill by remaining unswayed by externals. Similarly, in the *Tai-A Ki*, mushin enables a samurai to develop breadth of "vision" by remaining unswayed by particulars. These two texts project a distinct Zen message through a language familiar to the samurai. They were designed to develop samurai skill and character during a period of transition from war to peace by restraining the human ego and by indicating the common ground (discipline) between wartime and peacetime conduct.

However, at this point, a basic question arises: Zen (as well as Shingon Mikkyo) is a school of Buddhist thought that advocates noninjury, but swordsmanship is a practice designed to inflict injury. How can the two be reconciled? This question needs to be addressed, because, although Takuan did describe the manner in which the discipline of swordsmanship can be transferred to peacetime conduct, he did not present a rationale resolving this fundamental conflict.

Buddhism advocates noninjury* and stipulates adherence to the five precepts,† the first of which is noninjury. Zen, of course, observes the five precepts, but, contrary to popular notion, its ultimate aim is not enlightenment. Of course, Zen speaks of *satori*, a term that is popularly translated as "enlightenment." But *satori* etymologically does not mean enlightenment. It means "knowing the true self" (mushin). The purpose of Zen is to cultivate mushin, experientially,[19] through the "way"—what has previously been described as *do*. Where then is the *do*?

The *do* is not found in the realm of enlightenment; it is found in the realm of hell. Thus a popular samurai saying states, "fall into the pit of hell" (*meifu mado ni ochin*)—and find the true self within it. There is challenge (the cultivation of mushin) in the realm of hell, not in the realm of enlightenment.

This is not to say that the samurai sought after the art of killing. Yagyu Munenori spoke of the "life-rendering sword" (*katsujin-ken*) and the "death-rendering sword" (*satsujin-ken*). The former refers to a form of kama-e absent of an intimidating nature (i.e., enabling the opponent to exercise his skill without reserve and letting him withdraw graciously). The latter refers to the kama-e with an intimidating nature (i.e., not allowing the opponent to exercise his skills and defeating him mercilessly).‡ Munenori advocated the former.

---

* Noninjury, that is, *ahimsa*, is a term first used in the Upanisad, an ancient Indian text compiled in about 600–300 BCE. It is also a term indicated in the fourth item (right action) of the Buddhist Eight Noble Paths.

† The five precepts are (1) noninjury, (2) nonstealing, (3) no sexual misconduct, (4) no lying, and (5) no taking of intoxicants.

‡ Popularly, katsujin-ken and satsujin-ken are interpreted as the employment of the sword for worthy and unworthy causes, respectively. Here, I have interpreted them according to the Yagyu school. Both interpretations, however, are related.

But Jubei, Munenori's son, claimed that the lofy idea of "life-rendering sword" could be practiced only after having mastered "death-rendering sword." Jubei had a point: only after cultivating the skill to defeat an opponent would a swordsman be ready to practice "life-rendering sword." *Katsujin-ken* is a samurai term that was understood by those whose profession required them to be constantly exposed to death. It is this tragedy that triggered them to seek a new horizon of thought (katsujin-ken)—through the very discipline that led to that tragedy (satsujin-ken). Thus, heiho (martial art) is heiho (the art of peace), as Chosai has rightly pointed out.

Kendo Meditation

In kendo, meditation is observed briefly before and after practice. It is described in three categories.

PHYSICAL POSTURE AND BREATHING

Kendo practitioners are not professional meditation practitioners. They do not take the lotus position. They take the folded-knee posture (see fig. 3), which was the formal sitting posture of the samurai as well as of cultured people in the Tokugawa period. Even today, cultured Japanese sit on their matted floors in the folded-knee posture. But there is a subtle difference between the two postures, that taken by the cultured people and that taken by the samurai. Because the samurai were required to be alert at all times, their big toes on both feet were positioned close to each other—not overlapped or spread apart—so that they could be used to "spring up" in case of a sudden attack. The kendo practitioner today, therefore, uses this formal position in dojo (unlike the judo practitioner, for example, who sits with his feet folded in front). Aside from this subtle difference, kendo meditation posture is identical with that of Buddhists: the practitioners sit in an upright position (back straight, shoulders relaxed, chin up but placed close to the throat) with eyes closed (or half closed, the eyes then focused on the tip of the nose). Above all, they must breathe deeply, silently, and rhythmically, and preferably count numbers—for example, one to four—repeatedly. This kind of meditation is referred to as *ana-apana* in Sanskrit, *shu-hsi kan* in Chinese, and *susoku kan* in Japanese, that is, "counting-number-meditation." It is derived from the ancient yogic practice as a means to concentrate on numbers and thereby eliminating external distraction.

PURPOSE

For Mahayana Buddhists, the purpose of meditation* is twofold. First, it is to develop one-pointed concentration, to empty the mind, and to get rid of discursive thoughts. The kendo practitioner does the same in order to get rid of attachments. But whereas the Zen practitioner faces the wall to realize one-pointed concentration, the kendo practitioner faces the opponent to realize the same. Meditation as such is simply a ritual designed to establish the proper mind-set.

We have said that both Shingon Mikkyo and Zen have had considerable impact on classical kendo, but the goal of Shingon Mikkyo is to realize human-cosmos integration. Aren't the meditation schemes formulated by these two schools of Buddhism different? Only their expression is different. The ultimate goal of both schools is to cultivate direct cognition. That which has realized it is referred to as the true self. Technically, the true self in Shingon Mikkyo is referred to as *nyojitsu chi-jishin*, "knowing one's own mind, just as it is," cited in the *Mahavairocana-sutra*; in Zen it is referred to as *kensho*, "knowing the true state of mind," an expression cited by Hui-neng, the sixth patriarch. These two terms correspond to mushin.

---

* In early Buddhism, its practitioners engaged in meditation to realize nirvana. Etymologically, the term means "blowing out passion." It implied death, for one who is alive and kicking cannot be expected to completely blow out passion. In the context of Sino-Japanese Buddhism, nirvana refers to buddha-nature, that is, the

Mushin was previously described as the alternate state of consciousness. We now need to be more specific. *Mushin,* as the two terms cited above illustrate, actually refers to the "reconstruction" of the human consciousness—that which is absent of verbal fabrication, has become aware of the true self, and has developed the ability to exercise direct cognition.

Thus, although meditation, whether of Shingon Mikkyo or Zen, is usually practiced within the confines of a hall today, many skilled swordsmen practiced meditation in isolation, outdoors, often on a hilltop. In doing so, they faced the cosmos itself. In the clarity of this natural solitude, there is no intrusion of human scheming and calculation, of convention and intellectualization. Because the purpose of meditation is to look inside oneself, some also meditated inside a cave for prolonged periods—sometimes weeks—cutting themselves off from outside influence.

METHOD

Mushin was described categorically for the sake of convenience. These categories are actually conceived of as one discipline to be realized all at once. There is no time to pass through graded and fragmented states in the development of discipline when one is faced with an opponent who is ready to attack with lightning speed. To this extent, then, notwithstanding the fact that kendo meditation is designed to set the stage to realize mushin, it is not based on a gradual doctrine. It is abrupt. Even the term *mindset* is not just a preparatory stage to realize mushin. Actually, a practitioner goes through the gradual stage (establishing the proper mindset) and then realizes the abrupt, just like a college student who enters as a freshman, goes through graded stages of the educational process, and finally receives his or her diploma. At that time, what was gained

---

nature of the human consciousness that has realized the interdependence of all humankind.

through the gradual stage is distilled into wisdom, not fragmented knowledge. The impact of Shingon Mikkyo and Zen on kendo is pronounced because the meditation schemes both represent stem from an abrupt doctrine.

Take the case of one-pointed concentration in the context of kendo. It will be recalled that one-pointed concentration requires the practitioner to focus on the opponent. The question is, what part of the opponent? He should focus on the opponent's eyes. The eyes tell everything: the opponent's degree of alertness, his intent, and, most important of all, the moment of his charge. But he should not concentrate on these items in a sequential order. The practitioner, although focusing on one point, is aware of the totality of the situation. This concept—that all things are distilled in one point—is the basic characteristic of the abrupt doctrine.

3

The Development of Swordsmanship

The Historical Setting

THE HEIAN PERIOD spans the early ninth to late twelfth centuries, the Kamakura period the late twelfth to the mid-fourteenth centuries, the Warring States period the late fifteenth to the early seventeenth centuries, and the Tokugawa period the early seventeenth to the late nineteenth centuries. In this chapter, although references will be made to the late Heian and Kamakura periods, we are primarily concerned with the Warring States and Tokugawa periods for reasons that will subsequently become apparent.

Because the sword was one of the principal weapons employed by Japanese warriors throughout these periods, kendo is one of the oldest forms of Japanese martial arts. Of course, its roots can be traced to the legendary and early historical periods. But throughout these periods, swords were straight-edged,* and skills in swordsmanship were primitive. Slanted swords were developed sometime in the late Heian period (around the eleventh or twelfth century) based on the

---

* One of the oldest swords extant today is the Shichisei-ken (Seven Stars Sword), presumed to have been made sometime between the sixth and eighth centuries and preserved at the Ikku Shinto Shrine in Hatsuzaki, Nakamura City, in Aichi Prefecture. It is a straight-edged sword.

actual combat experiences of the samurai, contributing to the refinement of skills. Hence, popular notion claims that schools of swordsmanship developed in Heian, present Kyoto, in the form of Kyo-ryu (schools of the imperial capital), such as Gikyo-ryu, Ki-ichi Hogen-ryu, Gen-ryu, Kurama-ryu, and so forth. But these schools are not historically documented. The earliest historical documentation available is of schools founded in the beginning of the Warring States period, such as the Katori-ryu. Why?

The late Heian period represents a period of the rise of two major military clans, the Genji and Heike, who originated as the result of dynastic shedding. The Genji decisively defeated the Heike in 1185. During this period, martial arts were developed by the samurai in battlefields through individual efforts. The Kamakura period is characterized by the establishment of a distinctively samurai government, but as far as the history of martial arts is concerned, this is an extension of the previous period. The samurai in this period also developed martial arts skills through individual efforts. A radical change took place in the Warring States period: martial arts were systematized. When they were systematized, students sought masters and offered remuneration for their instruction. These masters or their students then began to record the lineage of their schools.

To examine the development of swordsmanship, therefore, it is necessary to describe the historical circumstances that led to the Warring States period, a period of total war that involved not only major military clans but the entire people of the country.

The Warring States Period (Late Fifteenth to Early Seventeenth Centuries): The Development of Combative Swordsmanship

Historical change is most distinctly evident when it is accompanied by a change in political power. In reality, however, it is the product of a gradual accumulation of forces germinating within the deeper layers of society that ultimately reveal themselves as a new power capable of overthrowing the old. Thus, although the Heian period represented the time of the glory of the Fujiwara aristocracy, the productive power of the land was actually held by the peasants, who, in previous times, fled the burden of taxation and the land to which they were bound. They sought refuge in the *shoen*, the manorial properties administered by the Fujiwaras who employed them. But the peasants gradually gained power and contributed to undermining the power that administered the shoen. In this socially unstable situation, the samurai challenged the Heian aristocracy and managed to establish their own government in Kamakura. But the process of dismantling the shoen continued up to the mid-fifteenth century, a process indicative of the peasants' latent power—and their capacity for violence.

Underlying the transition from the fourteenth to the fifteenth centuries was an advance in the means of production: iron farm tools were popularized, horses became widely used as sources of power, and the use of water mills brought about technical improvements in irrigation and farming. Increased farm production led to the rise of the merchant class, which facilitated the circulation of goods, contributed to establishing markets outside the shoen, and thus undermined the self-supporting shoen units of the aristocracy and their samurai guards. By the fifteenth century the peasants had consolidated themselves into village units and were managing themselves as independent tillers of the soil. Assuming greater prominence, they showed themselves eager to overpower their former superiors whenever they had the opportunity, and demands from above were no longer passively protested but vigorously resisted. Whenever authority still persisted, the peasants revolted. Peasant revolt produced economic chaos and undermined the established power.

The period from the late fifteenth to the late sixteenth centuries, therefore, represents a period of anarchy. The final collapse of central authority was triggered by the Onin Rebellion, which began in Heian in 1467 and continued for ten years. After this, war spread to the provinces. The daimyo (provincial lords), struggling to extend their economic influence, fought against one another and plunged Japan into a period of warring states that lasted for a century. It was also a time of revolt by the masses against established authority: emperors fought against aristocrats, aristocrats against the daimyo, daimyo against the samurai, and samurai against the peasants. Whether emperor, aristocrat, daimyo, samurai, or peasant, survival depended only on the strength and ingenuity of the individual. After the end of a century of war, the daimyo formed politically independent territories from their newly acquired economic spheres, swept away all vestiges of the old shoen, and successfully established a feudal society in which they exercised complete control over their territories and the people who lived in them. Many of these political leaders, the new daimyo, were former village headmen, who managed to overthrow the established daimyo during the chaos of 100 years of war. It was during this period, when rival military leaders zealously defended their own territory and covertly sought other territories, that there emerged samurai who were skilled in a variety of martial arts, in particular swordsmanship. These samurai used slanted swords.*

Slanted swords, which facilitated the development of swordsmanship, were already employed before the Warring States period, for example, in battles between the Genji and Heike clans in the late Heian period, in the subsequent battles that established the samurai government of Kamakura, and in battles between the Kamakura samurai and the Mongols in 1331–33. But it was not until the late fifteenth century that Iizasa Choisai, whom we have described in

---

* Japanese has a variety of words for swords. One is *tachi*. But the term *tachi* is written in different characters. Straight-edged swords used in the early historical, Nara, and early Heian periods are written as 大刀, while slanted swords used in the late Heian period and thereafter are written as 太刀. The employment of these two distinct terms is indicative of the evolution of Japanese swords from straight-edged to slanted. A few slanted swords and many *e-kotoba* (picture-word) paintings of samurai carrying slanted swords of the late Heian period are preserved at various museums throughout Japan, for example at the Tokyo National Museum at Ueno.

chapter 2, systematized and developed a school of swordsmanship based on his years of observation of combat. His school stimulated the rise of others in the years after his death. Subsequently, during the Warring States period, many eminent swordsmen appeared. The emergence of skilled swordsmen in this period, however, was not due only to internal historical circumstances but to external historical circumstances as well, namely, the introduction of firearms. Firearms were introduced by the Portuguese in 1543, and they radically changed military tactics.

Common sense suggests that in battles where firearms were extensively employed, swordsmanship would be outdated. But this was not the case. When swords, yari, naginata, and bows and arrows were the major weapons, samurai needed heavy armor. But firearms could penetrate any known armor, and so, reasoning that a direct hit from a firearm would be fatal, or at least immobilizing no matter what they wore, combatants preferred light armor. Light armor provided less defense but enhanced swordsmen's speed and maneuverability and made them more effective in hand-to-hand combat, which at that time was what decided the ultimate outcome of battles. The armor was in fact light enough that the samurai could wear it even on their way to the battlefield (except the helmet), unlike European knights who put their entire armor on only for the actual fighting.

During the Warring States period, then, firearms were used along with more traditional weapons. But it was the lowly foot soldiers who carried and used the firearms. It was the samurai, mounted on horses and trained in traditional martial arts, who led them and by their skills determined the battle's outcome. Daimyo of this period therefore sought to hire both men experienced with firearms and those skilled with swords. But ultimately, it was those daimyo who saw the advantage of firearms, and had the wealth and strategic geographic access to acquire them, who emerged as chief contenders in the struggle for military control of Japan.

For example, the use of superior firearms in the Battle of Nagashiro in 1575 enabled the combined forces of the Odas and Tokuga-was to defeat Takeda Katsuyori (1546–82).* In this battle, it is said that the Oda-Tokugawa forces employed 3,500 rifles aimed at 15,000 Takeda troops.† Of course, the defeat of the Takedas in the face of superior firepower did not in itself conclusively prove that swords, as well as other traditional weapons, were outdated. The samurai had to be trained not only in swordsmanship but also in handling bow and arrow, yari, and naginata and be skilled in *yawara* (proto-judo), sumo wrestling, horsemanship, and so on, because the order of bat-tles during this period began with shooting firearms and then arrows, and then, with the yari or naginata in hand, horse charges. If the yari or naginata broke, swords were used. If the sword broke, hand-to-hand combat was employed. When the opponent was overwhelmed, the samurai rendered the *coup de grace* to his opponent by cutting his jugular vein with the short sword. The opponent, particularly if he was a worthy one, was then beheaded. After the battle, heads were collected for display. The displaying of heads of worthy oppo-nents had three purposes: to confirm their death, to honor them, and to recognize the merits of the samurai who killed them.

Military tactics also underwent radical change during this period. In the late Heian period, in battles between the Genji and Heike, samurai fought as individuals: each opponent announced himself with dignity, proudly proclaiming the lineage of his family, its mili-tary accomplishments and his own, before engaging in combat. This type of ritual was observed even in the Kamakura period, up to the Mongol invasion (1275 and 1282). This brought about a radical change: the Mongols made no precombat announcements, went straight into battle with their short bows, and mounted whole armies

---

* Takeda Katsuyori was the son of the famous Takeda Shingen (1521–73), who was one of the most respected military strategists of the Warring States period and would most likely have succeeded in gaining military control of Japan had it not been for his early death.
† *Ran,* one of Kurosawa Akira's films, depicts this battle.

on horseback. The Japanese experience in battles with the Mongol hordes led to the development of army-level tactics.* But even at that, the final outcome of a battle was determined primarily with swords.

Thus, notwithstanding the introduction of firearms and change in military tactics, skills in swordsmanship and other forms of martial arts were still honored.† Although the variety of weapons used by the samurai of this period might be interesting, the late Donn Draeger has already dealt with this subject in an excellent manner.[20] Hence, here the focus will be on swordsmanship. In doing so we shall limit the discussion on eminent personalities who seem most representative of this period: Tsukahara Bokuden and Kozumi Ise-no-Kami, who lived in the early Warring States period; and Miyamoto Musashi and Ito Ittosai, who lived from the late Warring States period to the early Tokugawa period. The periods covered by these four men's lives have significance because swordsmanship, based on actual battlefield experience, was systematized during the Warring States period and refined during the early Tokugawa period.

Tsukahara Bokuden (1489–1571), popularly known as Bokuden, was born the second son to a family of Shinto priests in the service of the Kashima Shrine (in Hitachi, the present day Ibaragi Prefecture, not far from present-day Tokyo). Kashima traditionally honored a variety of martial arts, and Bokuden was exposed to that tradition by his father, Urabe Akikata. Bokuden was, however, subsequently

---

* The Genji and Heike did engage in army-level combat, including cavalry charges and sea battles, but at a smaller scale than those in the periods to follow.
† The daimyo of this period needed to construct castles on strategic sites, to promote effective administration, and to formulate strategies that were as much economic as military—to build roads and signal posts, reclaim land and develop agriculture, mine gold and silver, contract with merchants for arms and ammunition, and so on. As a result, although martial arts during this perod were referred to as *heiho,* implicit in that term was that the samurai with leadership capacity were expected to be knowledgeable in all these enterprises.

adopted by Tsukahara Yasushige because Yasushige, the lord of Tsukahara castle, had no son of his own. Both the Urabes and Tsukaharas were prominent families with a long tradition of martial arts. Bokuden's biological father and his adopted father were trained under Iizasa Choisai, whose wife was Bokuden's aunt.

Born and raised in families with an eminent martial arts tradition, Bokuden excelled in the use of a variety of weapons. At about the age of fifteen, he took to the road as a traveling swordsman, exposing himself to the dangers of attack by bandits and dueling. He ultimately conceived of what is known as the *hitotsu no-tachi*, literally the "one-slash sword." Details of this particular skill are not known, but it is presumed that "one slash" refers to a decisive first slash. His school is better known as the Shin-to-ryu, meaning that one confronts the opponent single-mindedly, without scheming or subterfuge.

Shin-to-ryu is a product of its time. It was designed for actual combat, not as sport kendo. It concentrates attacks to an enemy's vulnerable spots, such as the neck, the armpit, under the wrist, the crotch, and the thigh. Special attention was paid to techniques of slashing arteries and breaking joints. It did not attack those parts of the anatomy protected by armor or by solid skeletal structure like the head and the ribs, where one would have to slash repeatedly to deal a fatal blow. This school assumes that the swordsman is surrounded by enemies and so has time for only a single decisive strike at any one opponent before turning to face another.

Bokuden taught many outstanding students, such as Kitabatake Tomonoroi, the governor of Ise; Ashikaga Yoshiteru, the thirteenth Ashikaga shogun; and Matsuoka Myogosuke, who in turn instructed Tokugawa Ieyasu. But many of his students met untimely deaths. Kitabatake was attacked by the forces of Oda Nobunaga in 1569; he took up his sword and defended himself to the end, killing many of Nobunaga's men. Shogun Ashikaga Yoshiteru was betrayed by one of his generals. Forced to retreat inside his own residence, he thrust several bare swords on the floor to be used when a sword broke, but was subsequently overwhelmed and slain by superior numbers. These men developed too great a confidence in themselves, overlooking the fact that during the Warring States years, intrigue and betrayal were the way of life.

Bokuden himself is said to have engaged in battles thirty-three times,* and was wounded by arrows in six places. He engaged in duels seventeen times without defeat. The fact that he lived until the age of eighty-two attests to his skills in the art of self-defense. But these accomplishments in themselves do not reveal Bokuden's personality. Some popularly recounted episodes, whether fact or fiction, do tell us something about his character.

One day while traveling, Bokuden came to a river. He took a small ferry across and was accosted by a samurai boisterously telling the passengers of his exploits. He then faced Bokuden, who was sitting quietly at the other end, and asked what school of swordsmanship he had studied. Bokuden smiled and replied that his school was one that "defeats an opponent without arms [Mutekatsu-ryu]." Enraged, the swordsman challenged Bokuden to a duel. Bokuden, pointing to an islet in the river, directed the boatman to it. As the boat neared the islet, the samurai jumped to the shore, readying himself for the duel, and called upon Bokuden from the shore. Bokuden then took the boatman's oar, pushed the boat from the shore and left the samurai stranded.

Another story relates how Bokuden decided to test his three sons and select one as the official transmitter of his tradition. The test took place in his room. He placed a piece of wood on the door top

---

* During the thirty-three battles Bokuden engaged in, it is said that he beheaded 212 worthy opponents—a number averaging 6.4 kills per battle. This number might not seem significant. But battles in the early Warring States period did not employ weapons of mass destruction in great number. As previously stated, firearms were introduced in 1543, after the time when Bokuden, still young, was engaged in many battles. As such, to defeat enemies who wore protective armor was not an easy task.

so that it would drop as someone opened the door. The first son, sensing danger, stopped in front of the door, picked up the piece of wood, and then entered the room. The second son opened the door, but when the piece of wood fell he was able to dodge it. The third son opened the door and as the piece of wood fell, he sliced it with his sword. Bokuden transmitted the tradition to the first son. He had the ability to detect danger and avoid it. The second was reproached for not sensing danger and the third for not only not sensing danger but also for drawing his sword unnecessarily.

In yet another story, a group of Bokuden's disciples were walking along a road. The men passed a grazing horse, and the horse kicked one of the men. The man managed to dodge it, and his friends praised him for his alertness and speed. Hearing this, Bokuden remained silent. At another occasion, the disciples took Bokuden to the same road to see what Bokuden himself would do. Bokuden, having seen the horse from afar, urged his disciples to take another road.

To Bokuden, martial arts meant sensing danger before it strikes and avoiding it. If danger is unavoidable, then one should at least attempt to avoid violence. But if that too is unavoidable, then one should be prepared to defend oneself effectively—with one slash.

Today, Bokuden's Shin-to-ryu, popularly known as Bokuden-ryu, survives in Kashima, where its dojo is established within the shrine compound. But it is somewhat doubtful if the Shin-to-ryu is practiced there in an unadulterated manner. Interestingly, though, Shin-to-ryu also survives in Tsugaru in northern Japan, far from the site of its origin, under the name of Tsugaru Bokuden-ryu.

Kozumi (or Koizumi) Ise-no-kami (1508–77) belonged to the Kozumi family, who had traditionally been the lords of Ogo Castle in the present Gunma Prefecture. But during the time of Ise-no-kami's father, the family was defeated. After its defeat, Ise-no-kami served under Nagano Shina-no-kami, the lord of Minowa Castle, but subsequently left his new lord to further develop his swordsmanship. Ise-no-kami studied a variety of martial arts under Aishu Ikasai (1452–1538),* the founder of Kage-ryu, and he subsequently founded the Shinkage-ryu, or "new Kage-ryu." The meaning of the term *kage*, literally "shadow," remains obscure, but it probably refers to reflexive movements derived from conquering fear, doubt, and hesitation. Ise-no-kami was skilled in a variety of martial arts, but he was also a rational man and a compassionate one as well.† Three of his accomplishments are significant.

First, whereas swordsmanship had been practiced with bokuto (a hard wooden sword, as previously said), which could be lethal upon contact, Ise-no-kami invented the "bagged shinai" (*fukuro shinai*). The bagged shinai is made from thin split bamboo sticks and bound

---

* Ikasai was a native of Iga in central Japan. His background remains obscure. He traveled extensively, visiting Kyushu in the south and Kanto in the north in order to develop skills in a variety of martial arts. He is also said to have visited Ming China. How and where he developed his skills is uncertain. Samurai historians claim that he was a pirate. At any rate, in the scanty records describing his skill, he refers to the constant rhythm of the waves of the ocean—small waves ultimately developing into one big wave as they near the shore. Swordsmanship requires this kind of rhythmic and synchronized motion. But he also cites the stability of a mountain, the free movement of wind, and the reflexive actions of monkeys and other animals. He probably was an observant man, incorporating natural phenomena and animal behavior in developing martial arts skills. But more seems necessary to understand this man. The fact that he employed a variety of natural phenomena and animals in describing his arts might have been indicative that he was creating a swordsmanship version of totemism, not simply as a representative mark of his school but to symbolically describe the relationship between his school and natural phenomena, with the intent to incorporate the power of natural phenomena in the development of his art—just as Choisai incorporated cosmic energy in the development of his school. Some historians of swordsmanship, therefore, claim that whereas Choisai is the systemizer of martial arts of the Eastern (Tokyo and its vicinity) school, Ikasai is the systemizer of the same of the Western (Kyoto and its vicinity) school. Unfortunately, unlike Choisai's school, Ikasai's school is not documented.

† The leader in *The Seven Samurai*, one of Kurosawa Akira's movies, is a man who shaves his head, puts on a monk's robe, and rescues a child from an abductor. Ise-no-kami is the model for that character.

into a leather bag. It enabled the samurai to practice swordsmanship without major injuries and thus enhanced the development of swordsman's skills. Second, whereas swordsmanship had been taught experientially, he systemized it by assigning designations to a variety of skills and classified these skills into distinct categories. Third, because he described swordsmanship skills in a rational manner* he was able to attract outstanding men, such as Yagyu Sekishu, and thereby succeeded in transmitting his tradition. He stands in sharp contrast to Bokuden, who, though an accomplished swordsman, was not as successful as Ise-no-kami in transmitting his tradition. Thus, Shinkage-ryu of Ise-no-kami, transmitted through the Yagyus, has managed to survive even today. Bokuden's school also survives. But Yagyu-ryu is documented; Bokuden-ryu is not. Ise-no-kami's success in transmitting his school was not only the result of his skill in swordsmanship and his ability to systemize his skills, but also to his foresight to transmit his tradition. Furthermore, his compassionate attitude attracted samurai of gentle breeding.

There is an interesting episode related to Ise-no-kami. Once when Bokuden visited the dojo, where Ise-no-kami was under training as a young man, he found it difficult to evaluate Ise-no-kami's skill. Ise-no-kami was even-tempered. This aspect of his personality was reflected in his swordsmanship: Ise-no-kami was not intimidated by superior practitioners, but neither did he defeat opponents in an overwhelming manner. So it was difficult for Bokuden to tell whether Ise-no-kami had a skill superior to that of his opponent. Ise-no-kami probably demonstrated the sign of heijo-shin even as a young practitioner.

*   *   *

---

* The term *rational* is used here relative to Ikasai's system. Ikasai's description of swordsmanship was abstract, extensively using metaphorical expressions. Ise-no-kami's rational approach was recorded by Yagyu Munenori. (See *Heiho-kaden-sho* in Annotated References 12 and 13. For an English translation, see Annotated Reference 29.)

Miyamoto Musashi (1584–1645) was born in the village of Miya-moto in the province of Mimasaka (present-day Okayama Prefec-ture). His grandfather, Hirata Shogen, excelled in a variety of martial arts and served as the chief councilor of Shinmen Sadashige, the lord of Takeyama Castle. Musashi's father, Munisai (sometimes called Takehito), was also skilled in a variety of martial arts. His mother, Omasa, died soon after she gave birth to Musashi, and he was raised by Yoshiko, Munisai's second wife. But because of incompatibility, Musashi's father and stepmother subsequently separated.

Following the family tradition, Musashi, a youth of fierce temper, was trained in a variety of martial arts by his father. But he seemed to prefer Yoshiko's company to his father's. He spent most of his time at his stepmother's home. Yoshiko subsequently sent Musashi to Shoren-an, a Zen temple in Heifuku, a nearby village. Yoshiko's uncle presided at the tmple, and she hoped that the temple routine would temper Mushashi's personality.

It was at this time that Arima Kihei, a samurai experienced in duels, visited Heifuku village and posted a sign claiming that he would accept anyone who would challenge him in a duel. While returning from a calligraphy lesson, Musashi saw the sign, smeared it with his brush, and wrote that he would accept the challenge. The duel was scheduled for the following morning. But having heard this, Yoshiko's uncle was terrified. He called upon Arima and begged him to cancel the duel—telling him that Musashi was only a boy of twelve years old. Arima understood, but told the monk to accompany Musashi and explain to the audience the reason for the cancellation. The following morning, as the monk was about to make the an-nouncement, Musashi, armed only with a bokuto, stepped forward shouting words of challenge to Arima. Arima drew his sword, Mu-sashi leaped forward, threw away his bokuto, grabbed Arima, lifted him high above his head, and threw him to the ground. Before Arima could get up, Musashi picked up his bokuto and crushed Arima's skull.

This was Musashi's first duel. It is said that from the age of twelve to twenty-eight, Musashi engaged in sixty duels, always emerging victorious. The most significant duels were the ones with the Yoshika family (which transmitted the Kyo-ryu; see p. 43) in 1604, when Musashi was twenty-one, and with Sasaki Kojiro (who, it is believed, was trained in the Chujo-ryu; see p. 15) in 1612, when Musashi was twenty-eight. Of the two, the latter was most dramatic.

The duel, requested by Musashi, was to take place on an islet about two miles off the shore from a northern tip of Kyushu at 7:00 A.M. on April 13, 1612, in the presence of Lord Hosokawa's samurai, who acted as witnesses. Kojiro, accompanied by Hosokawa's samurai, appeared on time. Musashi did not. Spending the previous night at a boatman's home, Musashi had to be repeatedly summoned by the boatman to get up in the morning. He leisurely took his breakfast and then asked the boatman for an old oar. Dressed in simple attire, he finally got on the boat. The boatman feverishly worked on his oar while Musashi, totally unconcerned with time, slowly began to carve out a bokuto from the old oar. Kojiro, having seen the boat approaching the islet and having waited impatiently for hours, ran to the shore, throwing the sheath of his sword on the ground, and shouted words of accusation to Musashi for the delay. Musashi, with his headband (*tenugui*) tightly tied but completely relaxed, got off the boat, ignored Kojiro's accusation, and remained silent. Kojiro, with his long sword drawn, charged in. Musashi then shouted, "Kojiro, you are already defeated!" Burning with rage, Kojiro stopped for a moment, then took the aggressive jodan position and charged in again with the intent to cut through Musashi's skull. Musashi too leaped forward, targeting Kojiro's head. The witnessing samurai held their breath for, they thought, the weapons landed on the opponents at the same time. Musashi's headband was cut off, but it was Kojiro who fell to the ground.* Musashi looked down at Kojiro and took the zanshin position. Suddenly, Kojiro's sword swept through Musashi's feet, tearing Musashi's samurai skirt (*hakama*) a few inches. Musashi reflexively stepped back and then immediately leaped forward, this time crushing Kojiro's skull, blood pouring out from Kojiro's nose and mouth. Musashi dropped his bokuto and leaned over Kojiro to check his respiration. There was no breath. He picked up his weapon, bowed to the samurai witnesses, and left the islet.

What Musashi subsequently described in the *Gorinsho* (translated into English as the *Five Rings*)[21] reveals the psychological aspect of this dramatic duel. Its third chapter emphasizes mental calm and cautions one to avoid rage: Musashi remained calm, purposely delayed his arrival, and enraged Kojiro. Its fourth chapter speaks of "knowing the opponent": prior to his duel, Musashi had studied Kojiro's skill in using a long sword and hence carved out a long bokuto from the boatman's oar.

Musashi is one of the most colorful figures in the chronicles of samurai. Although an impetuous man in his younger years, his constant confrontation with death seemed to help him find a new horizon—that life is impermanent, and as such it should be honored. He left behind the *Five Rings*, which is an instructional manual on swordsmanship as well as his views on the life of a swordsman. The

---

* There is a samurai saying, "If one intends to capture a tiger's cub, go inside the tiger's den!" Swordsmanship requires charging forward and getting inside the opponent's range of defense, concerned neither with the opponent's charge nor with his weapon; otherwise one would not be successful in rendering a fatal blow to the opponent. What this means is that there should be only a fraction of an inch between the opponent's weapon and one's own body. It is this fraction of an inch that determines the outcome of a duel. After all, in a duel, the opponents are expected to be skillful swordsmen. A master swordsman would thus instruct his disciple, "Let the opponent cut your skin, but cut his flesh; let him cut your flesh, but cut through the marrow of his bone." It is with this kind of determination, a sutemi determination, that samurai engaged in a duel.

text does not represent an intellectual apprehension of life, but Musashi was by no means a nonintellectual. He wrote with style and had artistic sensitivity. He was a painter, calligrapher, and sculptor. He seemed to have realized mushin. His thoughts revealed in this text, however, are difficult to understand. They were derived intuitively and experientially, and the flow of logic, plus the choice of words and manner of expression, are all characteristic of the literary pattern of his age. The text cannot be understood in a linear, line-by-line and page-by-page reading, because Musashi was a mystic.[22] His thought went beyond the intellect into the realm of the intuitive. To understand his work we need to understand his life. But we are not concerned here with the life portrayed in his work. We are concerned with what is not portrayed.

Musashi's life from 1612 (the date of his duel with Sasaki Kojiro) until 1640—years covering Musashi's life from age twenty-eight to fifty-six—are not recorded. (There is one exception. Musashi visited his adopted son, Iori, who was in the service of Lord Ogasawara in Kyushu, in 1634.) These years reflect an individual's period of maturity on the one hand, and a period of transition from the Warring States period to the peaceful Tokugawa period on the other. It is very possible that Musashi sought peace during this period. But at the same time he probably was in great agony over the fact that although he was an accomplished swordsman, no one in a socially prominent position hired him. This issue needs elaboration, which is purely speculative.

Prior to 1640, what Musashi had realized was a realm grasped with the intuitive perception of a beast in the wilderness. Like the beast, Musashi discovered a realm in which there are no value judgments: a beast chases its prey to satisfy its appetite, and it is neither right nor wrong in doing so; when it is full, it no longer kills. Musashi did not worship violence but was perfectly at home with it. He was trained to kill, but he did not kill gratuitously or at random—just like the highly trained professional soldiers in elite military units such as the Green Berets and Navy SEALs, who are trained to kill and are at home with violence but detest meaningless violence. But the border between this type of warrior and a psychopath is vague. Both can be beastly, and their value judgment can be suspicious. We are not implying here that Musashi was a psychopath, nor that the elite groups mentioned above are psychopaths. Nonetheless, just like many war veterans in contemporary times who find it difficult to readjust themselves to peacetime activities, Musashi too seemed to have difficulty in adjusting himself to a new era of peace. Finally in 1641, Hosokawa Tadaaki, the lord of Higo in Kyushu, did hire him—when Musashi was fifty-seven years old. Tadaaki died the following year, and Musashi died three years thereafter. Although Musashi left the *Five Rings*, an impressive samurai text composed in complete isolation in a cave just before he died, it is possible to assume that he died feeling the futility of life. He never married.

At any rate, Musashi's swordsman tradition is popularly referred to as Nito-ryu, the school of two swords. It should be noted, however, that two swords were used in the Kyo-ryu as well as in the Shinkage-ryu. Nonetheless, it was Musashi who systemized the two-sword tradition. His school, however, is formally referred to as Niten Ichi-ryu, loosely translated as the "syncretic school." Although this school was transmitted to his disciples and his adopted son, it failed to survive. In today's kendo, rarely do we see a contestant employing two swords.

Ito Ittosai (1550/60–c. 1653) is the founder of Itto-ryu. The dates of his birth and death as well as the place of his birth remain uncertain. It is popularly believed that he was born on Oshima, an island about sixty miles south of Tokyo. Traditionally, Oshima was a site where criminals, including political offenders, were sent. Although the details of his parents are unknown, it is commonly believed that Itto-sai's father was either a political or criminal exile in Oshima and married a native.

As a child, he grew up in the Oshima wilderness, fishing, chasing animals, and shooting down birds with stones. Legend has it that one day he met an old man in the woods, who exposed him to the rudiments of swordsmanship and then subsequently disappeared.

At the age of thirteen, desiring to free himself from the isolated environment of Oshima and to make something of himself, he used a log to swim over twenty miles to the nearest point of the mainland peninsula. With his robust build, long hair, and shabby clothes, the natives of the peninsula called him Yasha (derived from the Sanskrit *yaksa*, "devil"). He lived at the Mishima Shrine, where he cleaned the yard and did miscellaneous chores. During this time a swordsman appeared at a nearby village. Yasha challenged and defeated him with a bokuto. Astonished, the shrine custodian presented Yasha with a real sword that had been offered to the shrine some years before. (Legend has it that this sword had been tied to the wall without its sheath, and in due time when the rope snapped, the sword cut through a huge, thick porcelain vessel on the floor.) Sometime thereafter, seven thieves entered the shrine, and Yasha killed them all with this sword. That made him locally popular. He left Mishima with the "vessel-cutting sword" and the blessings of the natives to further develop his skill as a swordsman.

As a young man, he took the name of Yagoro and was trained by Kanemaki Jisai, a swordsman of the Chujo-ryu (see footnote, p. 15) for about five years. By the end of the fifth year, his skill exceeded that of his master. He traveled, seeking superior masters by engaging in duels. It was about this time that he began to refer to himself as Ito Ittosai. There is a variety of exciting episodes about Ittosai during this period.

Ittosai was a womanizer and a heavy drinker. One summer night a group of men, whose master had been defeated in a duel with Ittosai, attempted to assassinate an intoxicated Ittosai while he slept with a woman under a mosquito net. The woman, hired by the assassins, removed Ittosai's sword from his bedside. But when the assassins cut off the strings of the net, Ittosai flung it at them and managed to take one of the assassins' swords. The assassins fled, and Ittosai named the skill acquired during this moment of danger as "the sword-abandoned technique" (*fussha-to*). This skill relies on ki-ai force and instant ma-ai reading alone. More importantly, this incident inhibited him from sleeping with any woman and indulging in heavy drinking.

In Kamakura, the ancient samurai capital, Ittosai vowed to visit the Hachiman Shrine for a hundred nights in the hope that Hachiman, the god of warriors, would offer him further insight into swordsmanship. On the last night, as he was about to leave the shrine, an assassin approached from behind. As the assassin was about to draw his sword, Ittosai intuitively drew his and slew the would-be assassin. He felt he had acquired the skill of direct cognition (*munen muso ken*, literally, "the sword of no-thought") and the reflexive ability to cope with unexpected challenge. The term *direct cognition* used here does not only refer to a state of mind absent the intrusion of intellect, as it was previously interpreted. It also refers to the instantaneous union of intuition and action. At any rate, it is said that Ittosai engaged in thirty-three duels.

As he aged, Ittosai sought out samurai to whom he could transmit his skills. He found two: Zenki, an uncouth former boatman with a robust build, and Mikogami Tenzen, a cultured samurai and a native of a village not far from the Kashima-Katori area. In all fairness to his most able disciples, Ittosai demanded that the two engage in a duel to settle the succession dispute. Tenzen slew Zenki, whereupon Ittosai offered his vessel-cutting sword to Tenzen and departed, saying that he had now abandoned the way of the sword and would seek the way of the Buddha. Like the old adage, "A samurai never dies, he just disappears," no account of Ittosai's life thereafter remains. After the duel, Tenzen took on the name of Ono Tadaaki, the alleged surname of Zenki, to pay homage to his former colleague whom he had slain. The Itto-ryu tradition was subsequently transmitted by Ono Tadaaki.*

Below is a summary of the history of swordsmanship as it developed in the Warring States period. It focuses on the four personalities— Tsukahara Bokuden, Kozumi Ise-no-kami, Miyamoto Musashi, and Ito Ittosai—described above.

What characterized these men is that they all lived in a violent period when survival depended on acquiring swordsman skills through battlefield combat, duels, or both. Furthermore, having mastered these skills, each sought a life of peace and tranquility, although whether they in fact acquired it is not the issue here. Ironically, they sought peace and tranquility through confrontation with death and violence.

Thus, both Bokuden and Ise-no-kami, while having experienced numerous battlefield combats, seem to have died with some degree of serenity in their old age. It is, however, doubtful whether we can say the same for Musashi, in spite of the fact that he did compose the *Five Rings*. In all fairness, the *Five Rings* does reveal considerable insight into integrating Buddhist thought and swordsmanship and demonstrates Musashi's stability of character. Nonetheless, what he

---

* The ryu transmitted by Tadaaki is called Ono-ha Itto-ryu, the Ono branch of Itto-ryu (hereafter referred to as Itto-ryu). Tadaaki, together with Yagyu Munenori, became the official instructor of swordsmanship to the shogun. But Tadaaki instructed even the shogun with uncompromising vigor and failed to receive the favor of the shogun. Thus, although both the Yagyu-ryu and the Itto-ryu had the sanction of the shogun, the shogun favored the former. Ironically, though, the favor extended to the Yagyu-ryu made that school the exclusive property of the shogunate, and its dissemination among those not in the direct service of the Tokugawas was prohibited. This circumstance limited the Yagyu-ryu and, in turn, contributed to Itto-ryu's popularity. And so, by the nineteenth century, a variety of schools—Nakanishi-ryu, Hokushin Itto-ryu, Muto-ryu (of Yamaoka Tesshu), and others—all emerged from Itto-ryu. And all have had considerable impact on modern kendo.

had composed may not project the sense of futility he felt. Thus, Musashi is an interesting and a controversial personality because both innate violence and the intellectual desire to suppress that violence seem to have coexisted within his mind.

As for Ittosai, he just faded away, probably contented with having found a disciple capable of transmitting his tradition and piously claiming that he now sought the way of the Buddha. He too is an interesting personality because, in contrast to other men who originated from eminent families, he was a son of an obscure political exile or perhaps of a banished criminal with no known family lineage. His success was probably due to a strong motivation to overcome this inferior social status. Ittosai exemplified the fact that mastering an art does not depend on family background and affluent social environment. It depends solely on individual motivation.

But most important, historically, is that Ise-no-kami systematized swordsmanship, attracted disciples of a rational nature, and was thereby able to transmit his tradition. Of course, Musashi composed the *Five Rings*, a swordsmanship text with a philosophical bent, and therefore, like Ise-no-kami, also systematized the swordsmanship of his own tradition. But whereas Ise-no-kami managed to transmit his tradition to the Yagyus, who in turn composed texts (see footnote, p. 53), Musashi failed to transmit his tradition in an effective manner.

But systematizing swordsmanship and transmitting that tradition are no indication of excellence in skill. Who among these four men, then, was the most skilled? There is no certain way to determine this issue because these men did not confront each other at the peak of their careers, and also because swordsmanship contests cannot be evaluated like modern sports in which objective records can be kept. Swordsmanship is one of those human activities in which skill is determined by gambling with death. What can be said with a degree of certainty is that although Musashi did engage in duels sixty times, he did not distinguish himself in battlefield combat.* And although Ittosai engaged in thirty-three duels, he never did take part in battlefield combat. It was Bokuden and Ise-no-kami who engaged in numerous battlefield combats.

Bokuden and Ise-no-kami lived in the early Warring States period. Musashi and Ittosai lived in a transitional period—between the late Warring States and early Tokugawa periods. This distinction is significant. Battlefield combat in the Warring States period required not only skill but also the strength to cut through armor. In contrast, in the early Tokugawa period, individual combat (duel without armor), which required speed and dexterity, was observed. The difference in design between collective and individual combats reflected the historical character of the time these two groups of men—Bokuden and Ise-no-kami on the one hand, and Musashi and Ittosai on the other—lived.

It is this historical shift—from collective combat to individual combat—that took place in the early part of the Tokugawa period on which we must now focus our attention. For it was during this period that swordsmanship was refined as an art. To this extent, then, the systematizing efforts of Ise-no-kami—in spite of the fact that he lived in the early part of the Warring States period—warrants attention, because it is his tradition, the Shinkage-ryu, transmitted by the Yagyus and referred to as the Yagyu Shinkage-ryu (or simply Yagyu-ryu, already discussed in chapter 2) that was most successful in the early Tokugawa period.

The Tokugawa Period: 1603–1868

Three outstanding daimyo emerged near the end of the Warring States period: Oda Nobunaga (1534–82), Toyotomi Hideyoshi

---

* Musashi took part in the Battle of Sekigahara (1600) and in the Shimabara Rebellion (1637–38). The former was fought between the pro-Toyotomi (Toyotomi Hideyoshi died in 1593), and the Tokugawa forces and signaled the doom of the pro-Toyotomi forces. The latter was a peasant's revolt that was quelled by the Tokuga-

(1536–98), and Tokugawa Ieyasu (1542–1616). Nobunaga, one of the greatest strategists of his time, attempted to destroy the military strength of other daimyo and to gain political control over all of Japan. His rise to power was, however, cut short when he was assassinated by one of his generals, Akechi Mitsuhide. Hideyoshi, a man of humble origin, defeated Mitsuhide and subsequently reigned as the supreme commander. After Hideyoshi's death, Ieyasu challenged the Toyotomi forces and, at the Battle of Sekigahara (1600) and subsequent battles in Osaka (1614 and 1615), defeated them. These battles marked the accession to power of the Tokugawas, who governed Japan from their capital, Edo, present-day Tokyo, from 1603 to 1868. We will focus our attention on the Tokugawa period, but because this period spans close to 300 years, we will divide these years into three periods: the early (seventeenth century), middle (eighteenth century), and late (nineteenth century) Tokugawa periods.

EARLY TOKUGAWA PERIOD (SEVENTEENTH CENTURY)

A strong government requires a firm economic foundation. Okubo Choan, in the service of Ieyasu, introduced the amalgamation process of extracting gold, a technique that found its way into Japan from Mexico. Ieyasu accumulated gold reserves and actively engaged in foreign trade. William Adams, an Englishman rescued from the Sea of Bungo in Kyushu, enlightened the Tokugawas with his knowledge of the West and contributed to the opening of trade with Holland and England. Ieyasu allowed Dutch and English ships free entry to the ports of Japan, negotiated with the Spanish officials in the Philippines with favorable results, and promoted trade with Southeast Asia.

Trade led to the arrival of Christian missionaries. Ieyasu initially gave tacit approval to missionary activities. He welcomed the Portuguese and Spanish merchants and often asked Catholic missionaries,

---

was. In the former, Musashi sided with the pro-Toyotomi forces but escaped; in the latter he sided with the Tokugawa forces, but his effort was not recognized.

whose integrity he undoubtedly respected, to act as commercial agents. Nonetheless, the benefits of foreign trade were his prime concern, and Christianity was, in his view, a necessary evil. It is alleged that he was influenced by the Dutch and English, who accused the Spaniards and Portuguese of harboring territorial ambitions, and claimed that Catholicism demanded loyalty to the papacy and thus posed a threat to the Tokugawas.

The Tokugawas were concerned with still another issue. Whereas the samurai in the Warring States period had the opportunity to be hired by daimyo, in the early Tokugawa period when peace was established, they did not. Hence, in the early Tokugawa period unemployed samurai (known as *ronin*) often rebelled, such as in the case of the Shimabara Rebellion (1637–38)—a major peasants' revolt assisted by ronin and Christians—and, on a smaller scale, the case of Yui Shosetsu and his group (1651). Moreover, the Tokugawas were gravely concerned with former Toyotomi daimyo and their samurai, who, although they had technically switched their loyalty, nevertheless posed a potential threat.

The Tokugawas, faced with these potential threats, were gravely concerned with internal security, and that concern gave rise to the establishment of an intelligence agency (*metsuke*) that provided the occasion for the rise of the Yagyu clan.[23] Because the Yagyu clan is our major concern here, its background needs to be discussed in some detail.

It is said that the Yagyu hamlet was first founded during the Taika Reform (645) and claimed as a shoen fief by Fujiwara Mototsuna in 885. Here, in 1038, Fujiwara Yorimichi established the Kasuga Shrine and enshrined the protective deity of the Fujiwaras. Also at that time, one Daizen Nagaie is said to have been sent by the imperial court to administer the territory. The Yagyus claim Nagaie as their ancestral root. Some five centuries later, in 1552, there was war between the two major clans—the Matsunagas and the Tsutsuis—who occupied the areas surrounding the Yagyu hamlet. The Yagyus, who had previously been defeated by the Tsutsuis, chose this time to revolt against them and succeeded. But they continued to maintain a precarious position as a minor power, siding with whichever army was successful. In the late sixteenth century, the Yagyu hamlet came under the jurisdiction of Oda Nobunaga. But more significant than this bit of historical background of this clan is the geographical setting of the Yagyu hamlet.

The Yagyu hamlet is isolated, surrounded by mountains, hidden in a deep ravine, accessible only through a narrow passage. It served as a convenient place for stragglers from battles. Over time the hamlet dwellers developed a distrust of outsiders, united against the established daimyo of lands around the hamlet, and dedicated themselves to wars of vengeance. This is all the more significant in light of the fact that the Yagyu hamlet is located ten miles northeast of present-day Nara and twenty miles southeast of Kyoto, the two ancient capitals, where wars were frequently fought.

Furthermore, the Yagyu hamlet lies near Iga and Koga, traditional training sites of the ninja. Ninja, popularly translated as assassins, were actually intelligence agents trained in the arts of self-defense, evasion, and survival, and as guerrilla fighters trained in the arts of stirring up disorder behind enemy lines. The typical ninja was familiar with arcane technologies, such as the use of explosives. Of course, they also played the role of assassins. Although the ninja tradition has been romanticized over the years, its actual history remains obscure because they were alienated from mainstream samurai society. It is questionable whether we can call the Yagyus a clan of ninja. But their hamlet's location near Iga and Koga, their isolation, their existence at the mercy of surrounding daimyo, and their focus on developing skilful swordsmen all suggest that they had some communication with the Iga and Koga ninja. Shunto-gozen, the wife of Sekishu (to be treated subsequently), came from the Okuharas, one of the eminent Iga families.

The Yagyus, however, were intelligence operatives of a higher order than the ninja. The Tokugawas did make use of known ninja, like Hattori Hanzo, an Iga ninja, who allied himself with the Tokugawas during the late Warring States period. But he and the group of men he commanded were hired simply as undercover agents during that period and were scattered soon thereafter. The Yagyus, by contrast, held positions of considerable prestige at least until the late seventeenth century, as head of intelligence.

Who then were the prominent Yagyu swordsmen? In the late Warring States period, the most notable Yagyu was the master swordsman Sekishu (1529–1606). The name Sekishu, literally "stone boat," is taken from one of his poems:

> Though one controls the rudder of military tactics,
> How hard a stone boat is to steer![24]

However skillful a swordsman Sekishu may have been, the poem indicates that he found it difficult to steer through the raging storms of political intrigue.

Sekishu was born in the Yagyu hamlet as the son of Yagyu Ieyoshi, a samurai in the service of Miyoshi Chokei, a local daimyo. Sekishu first served Chokei, but in 1563 he left Chokei to study swordsmanship under Kozumi Ise-no-kami and subsequently received certification. When Nobunaga became the supreme military commander, a piece of land illegally cultivated and possessed by the Yagyu clan was discovered and confiscated. Sekishu was forced into retirement. But in 1594, Tokugawa Ieyasu emerged as one of the major contenders for military power. And when Sekishu demonstrated his skills in swordsmanship, Ieyasu immediately became his student. By 1600, the year of the crucial Battle of Sekigahara when the Tokugawas defeated the main pro-Toyotomi forces, Sekishu was already in his seventies. He therefore sent one of his sons, Munenori, to the battle on his behalf. In honor of his service, Ieyasu returned the hamlet to the

Yagyus.* Sekishu died at the Yagyu hamlet in 1606, leaving behind five sons and six daughters. Two of his sons founded major branches of the Yagyu clan, one in Edo, and one in Owari, the traditional site of the Yagyu clan.

Yagyu Munenori was the head of the Edo Yagyus, became one of the two official instructors of swordsmanship to the shogun (see footnote, p. 61), and in 1632 was appointed as the head of the Tokugawa's intelligence.† He served with distinction under three Tokugawa shogun, Ieyasu (1542–1616), Hidetada (1579–1632), and Iemitsu (1604–51). His service to Iemitsu was outstanding because he was not only a skilled instructor in swordsmanship to Iemitsu but frequently advised him on political matters as well. And the successful role he played as the head of the Tokugawas' intelligence is attested to by the fact that after the suppression of rebels at Shimabara (see footnote, p. 63) and those led by Yui Shosetsu, no organized

---

* Ieyasu was not as simple-minded as this legend portrays. He probably became Sekishu's disciple and returned the Yagyu hamlet to Sekishu because he needed a loyal retainer to occupy the Yagyu hamlet, a strategic site near Kyoto, the imperial capital. Further, Ieyasu knew the close relationship between the Yagyus and the Iga ninja. In fact, it was through the Iga ninja that the Yagyus were able to collect intelligence information.

† Why was Yagyu Munenori rather than Miyamoto Musashi, both contemporaries, hired by the Tokugawas? Musashi aggressively sought duels. Munenori did not. In fact, the Yagyu swordsman tradition emphasizes defensive technique, then instantly transforming defense into offense. Thus, although both Musashi and Munenori composed impressive samurai texts, it is the work of the latter that commands enduring respect, because whereas Musashi's central theme was to defeat an opponent, Munenori emphasized the primacy of mind. The former is technically practical, the latter intellectually sophisticated. This difference, most likely, reflected their upbringings. As already said, innate violence and the intellectual desire to suppress it coexisted in Musashi. In contrast, Munenori was trained by his father, Sekishu, who in turn was trained under Kozumi-ise-no-kami, a samurai of a gentle breed. Furthermore, Munenori was influenced by Takuan, who emphasized the central theme of Zen, mushin, the primacy of mind, and contributed to building a samurai character appropriate for the period of peace. The Tokugawas were looking for a samurai leader who could tame the war-hardened samurai in the period of peace.

rebellion—with the exception of sporadic but sometimes quite intense peasant revolts—occurred until the nineteenth century.

Munenori had four sons and two daughters. His eldest son, Jubei (born in 1607), was the most accomplished Yagyu swordsman of his time. Jubei served under the second and third shogun but incurred the displeasure of Iemitsu in 1626 and left Edo, ostensibly to travel and further develop his skill as a swordsman. In 1638 he was pardoned and returned to Edo. But he never received the same degree of favor from the shogun as had his father Munenori.* Later Jubei retired to the Yagyu hamlet and died there in 1650 at the age of forty-two. One account says he died of a heart attack while he was hunting, another has it that he was poisoned.

Jubei's expulsion from Edo by Iemitsu might have been a ruse to distract daimyo, and perhaps Jubei was actually sent to the provinces as an intelligent agent and later poisoned by the men whom he had suppressed. The year that he was pardoned casts a suspicious light. It represented the time of the successful suppression of the Shimabara Rebellion. At any rate, Jubei's death marked the actual end of the family tradition of swordsmanship of the Edo Yagyus, although after Jubei's death, the Edo Yagyu tradition was transmitted to Munefuyu, Jubei's younger brother, and that tradition formally continued until the death of the family's last male heir in the early eighteenth century.

The other main branch of the family, the Owari Yagyus, had better success in passing on their tradition. They descended from Sekishu's eldest son, Shinjiro, who had three sons. The second, Toshiyoshi (also called Hyosuke, 1577–1650), was taught by Sekishu himself and excelled in swordsmanship. Toshiyoshi transmitted the Owari Yagyu tradition. Sekishu's official choice of Toshiyoshi to carry on the Yagyu tradition seems to indicate that he did not look kindly upon his son Munenori, who was deeply involved in Tokugawa politics.

---

* It seems that Jubei did not get along with Munenori, his father. He preferred the Owari Yagyu tradition rather than that of the Edo tradition.

Although Toshiyoshi was Sekishu's choice to carry on the family tradition, Kato Kiyomasa, a powerful daimyo in Kyushu in southern Japan, asked for his service, and Sekishu reluctantly gave in. While Toshiyoshi was in Kato's service, he was sent to suppress a peasant revolt. The brutality of this suppression, with its murders of unarmed women and children, was something Toshiyoshi was unable to take. He immediately left Kato's service and trained himself further in swordsmanship. He was primarily active in the period of peace that followed the Warring States years.

Toshiyoshi revolutionized swordsmanship. During the Warring States period, brute strength to cut through armor was required, but during peacetime, when the samurai wore no armor, speed and dexterity were required. For example, he emphasized the high-level jodan position, which was not effective when the samurai wore helmets and shoulder plates during the Warring States period, but was extremely effective when they wore no armor during the period of peace. (To this extent, he laid the foundation for the development of modern kendo.) Furthermore, he, like many other skilled swordsmen, disciplined himself in Shingon Mikkyo and Zen to nurture direct cognition, and was therefore able to instantly read the opponent's intent. He made use of this ability to master Muto-ryu (see p. 15). Muto-ryu was initially conceived by Kozumi Ise-no-kami and transmitted to Sekishu, who in turn transmitted it to Toshiyoshi. It constituted one of the most sophisticated skills of the Yagyu tradition because it required one to perceive the opponent's intent instantly, and, at the moment of the opponent's attack, lunge in and block him body to body. Meditation provided these qualities of alertness, speed, and, most important of all, freedom from attachment to the opponent and the opponent's weapons. (See pp. 78–80 for further details on the Muto-ryu.) Toshiyoshi eventually served under Bishu Yoshitoshi, an eminent daimyo related to the shogun. He died in 1650 at the age of seventy-two, and the Owari Yagyu tradition was then transmitted by his sons, one of whom was Renyasai, the most skilled swordsman of his time.*

In sum, then, the Yagyus emerged as a prominent clan in the early Tokugawa period because, first, it gave birth to Sekishu, a skilled swordsman who transmitted Ise-no-kami's Shinkage-ryu; second, Munenori, the son of Sekishu, became an official instructor to the shogun, head of the Tokugawa intelligence, and, under the instruction of Takuan, integrated Zen and swordsmanship; and third, Toshiyoshi, the grandson of Sekishu, conceived of a new style of swordsmanship.

MID-TOKUGAWA PERIOD (EIGHTEENTH CENTURY)

In 1639 the third shogun, Tokugawa Iemitsu, forbade Portuguese vessels to enter the ports of Japan. Thereafter, only the Dutch were allowed to enter Deshima, a man-made island in Kyushu. That year marked the beginning of a period of Japanese political isolation that was to last for the next 214 years. The policy of isolation obstructed the growth of international trade and commerce and excluded external influence that might have further broadened and enriched Japanese culture.

The effect of policy on society and subsequently on its citizens is

---

* Although the Edo Yagyus managed to be recognized socially and politically (Munenori was elevated to the rank of daimyo), it was the Owari Yagyus who actually transmitted the mainstream Yagyu swordsman's tradition. Once, Iemitsu, the third Tokugawa shogun, instructed Munefuyu (Munenori's son and the legitimate transmitter of the Edo Yagyu tradition) and Renyasai (Toshiyoshi's son and a representative of the Owari Yagyu tradition) to engage in a bokuto duel. Munefuyu was defeated. It might also be mentioned that although both the schools of swordsmanship of Yagyu Munenori and Ono Tadaaki had the official sanction of the Tokugawas, it was the Owari Yagyu tradition, in particular, that developed by Yagyu Toshiyoshi, which proved revolutionary. That is, whereas the swordsmanship traditions at both Yagyu Munenori and Ono Tadaaki did represent schools of the transitional period from battlefield combat to duels, Toshiyoshi specifically emphasized speed and dexterity and illustrated in concrete form the swordsmanship of the time.

generally felt after it has been established by the state. The sociopolitical ideology that shaped Tokugawa policy was neo-Confucianism, in particular that of the Chu-tzu school. Based on this school, propriety was clearly defined and dictated all aspects of life. The development of a progressive spirit was curbed, and an extremely formal and fragile culture, warped in the direction of extreme hierarchical stratification, was created. Thus members of that society took a domineering attitude toward their inferiors and a timid and submissive one toward superiors. The effect of isolation and of the Chu-tzu school shaped the social character of eighteenth-century Japan.

Nonetheless, the Tokugawa policy of isolation contributed to establishing sociopolitical stability, and the Chu-tzu school provided the rational ground for enforcing law and order. Stability and law and order gave rise to the merchant class. And the rise of the merchant class in turn created new forms of entertainment for the pleasure-loving city people of Edo. Light haiku poetry, novels, puppet and kabuki plays, and *ukiyo-e* painting were all popular. This affluent and urban culture shaped the swordsman's tradition of the mid-Tokugawa period.

By this time, the emphasis in swordsmanship was on theory rather than skill; on codified discipline rather than the spirit of laying one's life on the line. Prohibitions on tests of skill by duels or by contests between different schools provided the opportunity for hundreds of schools to emerge, because there was no objective way of determining which was better than another. In these dojo, kata (prearranged stylized form practice) rather than combat practice was the dominant form of training exercise. Kata exercises were required for three years, sometimes even for seven years, before combat instruction took place. Many students abandoned swordsmanship because practice based only on kata was uninvigorating.

The kata of the mid-Tokugawa period were refined to the point that they produced swordsmen whose style resembled that of an actor of a *wakashu* kabuki play. The swordsmen's kata of this period can be compared to method acting of Western theater, which emphasizes entering into the mindset and motivation of the character. Similarly, in kata, the practitioner repeated set sequences of attack and defense while trying to visualize as strongly as possible his imaginary opponents.

Here it should be noted that the *ma-zumori* (*ma*-evaluation), developed during the previous period by many schools of swordsmanship, referred not to a pattern of movement but, integrated with kama-e, referred to a mental attitude (as was described in chapter 1). Of course, kata in swordsmanship is essential in that it establishes the basic repertoire, just as in the exercises of classical ballet. But an overemphasis on kata, not supplemented with actual confrontation with an opponent, can stifle the practitioner's creativity and mold him into a purely aesthetic figure. Swordsmanship in this case is a ritual referred to as *keho* or (*kaho*), stylized swordsmanship.*

The decline of realistic swordsmanship and the development of

---

* In contrast, during the Warring States period, swordsmen developed their skills by isolating themselves in mountains and hitting trees and boulders with bokuto. They roamed the hillsides to strengthen their legs and balance, chopped kindling to strengthen their wrists and arms, ate what they gathered from the natural environment, and meditated in the open to realize body-mind integration. Through these forms of discipline they eventually developed kata appropriate to their own personalities and established independent schools of swordsmanship. Kata was not standardized at this time. Nonetheless, although swordsmanship declined in both prestige and practice in the eighteenth century, there were exceptions. For example, Mariya Enshiro (d. 1742), who transmitted the Sekiun-ryu (a tradition which strongly emphasized the primacy of the mind), is said to have engaged in contests hundreds of times without being defeated. And Hirayama Gyozo (b. 1759), who was born into an Iga ninja family and was the founder of Chuko Shingan-ryu (a subschool of Shingan-ryu), enforced combat practice, equipped his students with short bokuto, forced them to charge in, and cultivated alertness, speed, and the instantaneous reading of ma-ai. Gyozo was also a learned man. He submitted to the Bakufu essays pertaining to the defense of the Japanese northern frontier. Although the Bakufu rejected his ideas, nonetheless, it subsequently urged the northern daimyo to survey the northern terrain, to investigate the activities of the Russians, and to prepare for its defense.

stylized kata in the mid-Tokugawa period prompted conscientious swordsmen to devise new instructional methods, which led to the development of the bogu, protective armor designed for practice. Yamada Heizaemon, the founder of the Jiki Shinkage-ryu, together with his son, Naganuma Shirozaemon, invented the earlier bogu, which became the model for the present bogu. Naganuma also improved Ise-no-kami's bagged shinai and invented the prototype of the shinai used today. The Nakanishi school, an offshoot of Itto-ryu, invented the do, the protective gear for the torso made out of bamboo slats threaded together. Some swordsmen criticized the wearing of bogu as a sign of timidity, but the popularity of the bogu continued to grow.

As the merchant class increased in power, city people flocked to dojo that used protective gear. They did so because swordsmanship was more interesting, invigorating and creative when practiced with bogu in actual confrontations, rather than simply observing kata exercises. But swordsmanship with bogu was conceived of primarily as a sport, rather than as a way of developing skills useful in combat, a phenomenon characterizing the peaceful and affluent mid-Tokugawa period.

LATE TOKUGAWA PERIOD (LATE EIGHTEENTH TO MID-NINETEENTH CENTURY)

The affluence of merchants cast the peasants into the depths of poverty, and because the Tokugawa economy was dependent on the labor of peasants, the poverty of the peasants threatened the country's economy as a whole.* Furthermore, the mid-nineteenth century encroachment of Western colonial powers in Asia—the Sepoy Mutiny in India; the Opium War in China; the invasion of countries

---

* It is estimated that there were over 3,200 peasant revolts during the Tokugawa period, clearly indicating that the Tokugawa policy of maintaining urban prosperity was sustained at the expense of suppressing the peasants. The number of annual revolts increased as the Tokugawa period neared its end.

in southeast Asia; the Russians posing a potential threat to Japan's northern frontier; and Commodore Matthew Perry of the United States with his four "black ships" demanding that Japan open its ports—all contributed to political instability. Economic and political instability gave rise to anti-Tokugawa factions that identified themselves with the emperor. In the late Tokugawa period, then, the samurai took up arms to defend their territories from peasant uprisings, from foreign powers, and from each other, and led them to recognize the need for serious training in swordsmanship.

But the art could not have been revived so swiftly had it not been for the tradition maintained—although precariously, to be sure—during the previous period. Furthermore, granted that swordsmanship had become sterile and stylish rather than combative as the result of emphasis on kata exercises, and sportive as the result of the development of protective gear, still the effect on swordsmanship of the influx of energy associated with the development of urban folk culture during the previous period cannot be ignored. Many skilled swordsmen of this period were in fact of nonsamurai origin. For example, the two skilled swordsmen of the Shindo Munen-ryu, Saito Yakuro and his top disciple, Busshoji Yasuke, were of peasant origin. Kondo Isamu and Hijikata Toshizo, the leaders of the Shinsengumi (Tokugawa-hired security force in Kyoto), were also of peasant origin.

Here we will deal with three prominent swordsmen: Chiba Shusaku, Yamaoka Tesshu, and Sakakibara Ken'kichi.

Edo was the mecca of swordsmanship in the early nineteenth century. The three major dojo in Edo of this time were managed by Chiba Shusaku, Saito Yakuro, and Momoi Shunzo. Prominent political men of the late Tokugawa period and early Meiji period emerged from the dojo of these men.* Of the three major dojo leaders—

---

* For example, Sakamoto Ryoma (assassinated in 1867, a year before the Meiji Restoration), Kiyokawa Hachiro, and others emerged from the Chiba dojo; Katsura Kogoro (later known as Kido Koin), one of the distinguished statesmen of the Meiji

Shusaku, Yakuro, and Shunzo—Shusaku was most outstanding, not because he was the most skillful swordsman of the time but because he demonstrated skill in the management of his dojo and in promoting the popularization of swordsmanship.

Chiba Shusaku (1788–1855) was born to a family of peasants in the hamlet of Hanayama in Rikuzen (the present day Miyagi Prefecture) in northern Japan. Another account says that his father was a skilled swordsman in the service of the Somas, a clan in northern Japan, who became a peasant when he resigned his position to be free of bureaucratic chores. Details of Shusaku's origin remain obscure, but what is certain is that he was raised in an atmosphere free from the restraints of the samurai code, and roamed the open spaces of his native territory playing at battle with his peers. Although mired in poverty, his father had high expectations for his son. At the age of sixteen, Shusaku was introduced to Asari Matashichiro, originally a humble clam peddler (*asari* means "clam") who had become a skilled swordsman and transmitted the Nakanishi-ryu tradition. Asari was then living in Matsudo (currently a suburb of Tokyo). After some seven years of training at the Asari dojo, Shusaku received his certification and was adopted by the Asari family. He married Asari's adopted daughter and took the family name with the intent of carrying on the Asari family tradition. But differences of opinion on matters of instruction and dojo management developed between Matashichiro and Shusaku. As a result Shusaku left the Asari dojo for Edo, where he systematized his own school of swordsmanship. He identified it as the Hokushin Itto-ryu. At the age of twenty-three, he opened a modest dojo at Nihonbashi in Edo. There were some 300 dojo in Edo at that time, and competition for students was intense. In the innovations that led to his success, Shusaku demonstrated his skill at administrative strategy.

---

government, emerged from the Saito dojo; and Takeuchi Han'heita emerged from the Momoi dojo.

Swordsmanship in a commercial sense is a commodity to be sold to students. Shusaku's swordsmanship was high-quality merchandise, but more than that, he made extensive use of the popular protective equipment. He also recognized the need to gain control of the channels of distribution of his merchandise. He sent his eminent students to visit various clans, calling on the daimyo to send students to his dojo and assuring them that their samurai would be properly trained. He also ignored social status and extended an invitation to the common citizens of Edo to practice at his dojo. Finally, as a means to motivate his students, he gave periodic examinations and awarded degrees of rank—not in itself a novelty, but whereas other dojo awarded about ten ranks with a "gift-payment" required for each, Shusaku saved his students money by establishing only three. But most importantly, he was careful to maintain the high quality of his merchandise: he frequently required students to practice on a floor sprinkled with beans to develop proper footwork (no hopping but slide-leap straight forward with both feet on the floor) and stable stance (go forward from the hip); encouraged practice with multiple opponents simultaneously to develop awareness of angles of attack and to instantly transform defense into offense; and emphasized attack, not the kind normally practiced through kata, but a continuous slashing and thrusting aimed to develop openings and then deliver a decisive blow.

In 1825 Shusaku's dojo, called Genbukan, was transferred to Otamaike in the heart of Edo, and so was then called the Otamaike dojo. It is said to have occupied 10,000 square meters of space, with some 3,500 students registered at one time. Shusaku is said to have trained some 6,500 students during his lifetime. (The tradition of his school still survives today, and the Genbukan, smaller now, is located in the Suginami Ward in Tokyo. Many of its students are now housewives who assemble there during the day, practically every day, putting in some three hours of practice.) The Hokushin Itto-ryu, like the

Nakanishi-ryu, has had considerable impact on the formation of modern kendo.

Yamaoka Tesshu (1836–88)[25] was a respectable *hatamoto*, a samurai in the direct service of the shogun in Edo. Although initially trained in the Chiba dojo,* he systematized Muto-ryu (the no-sword school).† The term *no-sword school* can be misleading because only after strenuous training can one hope to face an opponent successfully without a sword.

A novice who entered Shunpukan, Tesshu's dojo, was not exposed to the fundamentals of kendo—how to hold the shinai, how to swing and thrust a shinai, how to position the feet to maintain the proper stance, how to defend himself, and so on. No verbal instruction was offered. Instead he faced his superior, who mercilessly attacked; when he was out of breath, a crushing body-blow would follow until he was finally thrown to the floor. Nonetheless, in due time, a novice would acquire the skill to hold the shinai properly and to render the effective "snap," and would learn through body-blows that the best defense is an offense, and that the most effective offense in the face of an intimidating opponent is a go-for-broke sutemi attack.

Tesshu emphasized the primacy of mind—disciplining the mind over developing physical skills. Thus, *tachikiri shiai*, endurance practice, characterized the Shunpukan's norm of practice. First, the practitioner faced ten senior practitioners who challenged him one-to-one continuously from early morning until late afternoon with only one break for a simple meal (rice gruel and pickled plum) swallowed

---

* Shusaku's younger brother as well as his son also administered independent dojo. After Shusaku's death, many students trained themselves at one of these dojo. I refer to them collectively as the Chiba dojo.

† Muto-ryu was previoulsy described with reference to the Yagyu-ryu. But whereas Yagyu-ryu's Muto-ryo is derived from Kozumi-Ise-no-Kami's Shinkage-ryu, Tesshu's Muto-ryu is derived from Itto-ryu. What both schools aim at is, however, identical: to disarm an opponent without a weapon.

without taking off his bogu (of course, taking off the helmet). The second consisted of the same kind of practice for three days, with time off for simple meals and sleep. The third also consisted of the same kind of practice but lasting for one week. The first consisted of 200 practices, the second 600, and the third 1,400. If these numbers were not fulfilled, neither break nor sleep was permitted. These students literally dragged themselves to the dojo, and those who survived those strenuous practices were not only bruised and completely exhausted, but would find blood in their urine and excrement. Even when asleep, the novice constantly dreamed of practice, and some were unable to distinguish between dream and reality. Only the survivors of such tests were given the Muto-ryu certification, a certification that assured them that they were capable of defending themselves without a sword.

His students faithfully observed these practices, for Tesshu did not enforce discipline that he himself did not observe. He was not only a disciplinarian but also an ascetic. His daily routine was to get up at five, engage in kendo practice from six to nine, practice calligraphy from noon to four, and engage in Zen meditation at night for several hours until two AM.

His greatest achievement took place just prior to the Meiji Restoration, when he served as a liaison between the Tokugawa and the imperial forces, and thus was instrumental in preventing the city of Edo from becoming a battleground. To do so, he had to penetrate deep into government-held territory to see their leader, Saigo Takamori. This was no easy task. Subsequently, after the Meiji Restoration, despite his being a Tokugawa hatamoto, he skillfully adjusted himself to the changing political situation and served the new government with distinction. He channeled medieval loyalty to the newfound government and became a confidant of the new emperor (Emperor Meiji). But more important than his political view was the switch he made in the manner of training his students.

Tesshu transmitted the Ito Ittosai's Itto-ryu tradition. But his

Muto-ryu was a development over Ittosai's school. This does not mean that Tesshu's skill was superior to that of Ittosai. It means that Tesshu was aware of the changing value of the early Meiji period and channeled the discipline acquired in his dojo to effectively respond to the needs of the new society bustling with the sound of modernization. He instructed his students not to be swayed by external distractions and to maintain composure and self-confidence at all times. However we might evaluate his sociopolitical stance—switching his loyalty and adjusting to a new era—Zen shaped his personality. For example, although he suffered from painful stomach cancer, he never revealed his pain to others. And it is said that several days prior to his death, he provided his last kendo practice to his students, demonstrating a vigor unmatched by his students. On the day of his death, with the help of his wife, he took his last bath, cleansed himself, put on the white ceremonial robe in preparation for his death journey, and bade farewell to his friends and students on a sweltering summer day. A picture portraying him at the time of death—sitting in a meditation posture and holding a fan—is still extant.

Sakakibara Ken'kichi (1830–94), born thirty-six years after Shusaku and a contemporary of Tesshu, was another eminent swordsman of the late Tokugawa period. But whereas Shusaku succeeded in popularizing swordsmanship with his managerial skills, Ken'kichi was a loner; and whereas Tesshu succeeded in adjusting himself to social changes brought about by the new period, Ken'kichi did not. It was his misfortune to live well past the Meiji Restoration, into the period when the wearing of swords was prohibited and when rationalism, rather than the samurai value system, was honored. Furthermore, he was a low-ranking retainer of the Tokugawas, and their defeat left him without a master or a stipend, although he was in all probability the most accomplished swordsman of his time.

Ken'kichi took up swordsmanship at the age of eleven. He was trained under Odani Seiichiro (1798–1864), a prominent swordsman of the Jiki Shinkage-ryu, and received his certification in his twenties. This is considered a late age for a skilled swordsman to receive certification, particularly for one who took up swordsmanship so young. But there was a reason. Receiving certification required a substantial payment to the master. And the disciple, by tradition, had to provide a banquet for his master and colleagues. Ken'kichi was too poor for such extravagances. So his master finally allowed Ken'kichi to receive certification without payment and footed the bill for the banquet.

In 1853, Commodore Perry's forced entry into the port of Uraga to open up Japan so alarmed the Tokugawas that they urged the samurai to improve their swordsmanship. Ken'kichi was invited to become a swordsmaster of the Tokugawas' Kobusho, the training center for martial arts. Furthermore, he established a dojo at Kurumazaka in Edo in 1864. This signaled the peak of his career. He was also appointed personal guard to Iemochi, the fourteenth Tokugawa shogun (1846–66), who died of an ailment in Osaka, leaving Ken'-kichi with no lord to channel his loyalty. In the old samurai tradition, a samurai has only one lord.

The Tokugawas were defeated in 1867 and retired to Shizuoka, about 150 miles west of Edo, taking with them some 8,000 retainers, including Ken'kichi. The population of Shizuoka at that time was approximately 35,000, so there were no adequate accommodations for all the Tokugawa retainers. Some set up shops, but all of them failed.

Eventually, Ken'kichi returned to Edo, now renamed Tokyo, and reopened his dojo. His friends, now ronin, visited him to talk, eat, and drink. The dojo was constantly in a state of poverty. At this time, Ken'kichi was contacted by Shimmon Tatsugoro, a local head of construction workers,* who had taken a liking to Ken'kichi. The two

---

* One of the major catastrophes of ancient Edo was fire, which easily spread over an extensive area because houses were then constructed with flimsy wooden frames. Hence, as early as 1650, groups of firefighters (*hikeshi*, sometimes also referred to as

subsequently organized a new business: demonstrations of swordsmanship for the purpose of public entertainment. Although they
were initially successful, the city folk eventually took to other forms
of entertainment. Ken'kichi never cared for the business in any case.

Ken'kichi was the last samurai of the feudal age and represented
the cream of classical kendo. He was upright and unbending. He
knew honor and shame. But he apparently died a frustrated man, for
the samurai values in which he had been nurtured were no longer
felt to be valid in this time of change. But he was not a rebel. He
refused to take part in one of the last resistance movements
launched by the pro-Tokugawa Shogitai in Ueno in Tokyo. It was
perhaps this kind of personality—one who refused to accept the values of a new society and thereby displayed no ambition whatsoever
to realize upward mobility under the new government, who remained
loyal to the Tokugawas but did not revolt against the emperor, and
who quietly suffered the agony of his own consciousness—that
seems to have attracted Dr. Erwin Baelz (1849–1927),[26] a German
who came to Japan in 1878, taught pathology at Tokyo Imperial University, and lived in Japan for the next twenty-nine years. Baelz was
a student at Ken'kichi's dojo, where the most severe kind of training
of that time was observed. He reported that there were always several
students lying on the floor as a result of concussion when Ken'kichi's
shinai landed on their heads, and that students constantly bounced
their heads on the dojo pillars in an attempt to train themselves to
withstand these blows.

We have focused on these three samurai—Chiba Shusaku, Yamaoka
Tesshu, and Sakakibara Ken'kichi—not only because they were

---

jo-hikeshi) were organized. Their members consisted of civilians led by samurai. In
1718, the firefighters were divided into forty-seven groups, many of whom were
construction workers who worked as firefighters at times of emergency. Shinmon
Tatsugoro was a civilian head of one of these groups. He is therefore sometimes
referred to as a civilian head of firefighters or a local head of construction workers.

skilled swordsmen, but also because Shusaku and Tesshu demonstrated that it is not primarily swordsmanship that counts in the game of human survival, but the ability to read and adjust to sociopolitical changes. The discipline cultivated through swordsmanship has no meaning at a time of peace if that discipline cannot be applied to the realities of the time. Shusaku, with his managerial skills, showed that he was keenly aware of societal needs and could respond to them most effectively. Tesshu, although by temperament not a polished statesman of national stature, nevertheless was sensitive to political changes and thereby left his own legacy. Ken'kichi was an upright, disciplined, perhaps too honest man, but he was incapable of properly reading sociopolitical changes and making the necessary adjustments. Shusaku and Tesshu were popular samurai figures of the late Tokugawa period; Ken'kichi, although probably the most accomplished swordsman of the three,* was not. And because he was not, there is an element of pathos surrounding his personality, a personality that dauntlessly refused to accept the values of the new era.

What then were the ancient values of the samurai? And in what manner were these values demonstrated? These questions now lead to an examination of bushido, the code of the samurai. To do so, we need to look back in order to contextualize bushido historically.

---

* Ken'kichi's great skill was attested to in 1879, slightly over ten years after the beginning of the period of modernization of Japan. At that time, the Japanese national police forces decided to train their officers in kendo. Ken'kichi was appointed to evaluate and select kendo instructors for the central police academy.

4

The Development of Bushido, the Code of the Samurai

The Historical Development of Bushido

SINCE *BUSHIDO* MEANS "the way of the samurai," the term *samurai* first needs to be clarified. If *samurai* is defined as warriors employed for the defense of the community, like those in prehistory who served the Yamato clan in its territorial expansions, or those of the early historical period who served as guards to the aristocracy, then the samurai, like warriors in any other society, have their origin in very early times. But in prehistorical and earliest historical times, Japanese warriors existed under a political system governed by the aristocracy, during which time they did not develop a distinct identity. Only when powerful warriors emerged as the guardians of manorial properties in the provinces, when strong allegiances developed among the retainers to these warriors, and when their respective positions became hereditary, did the social status of the samurai become distinct. Their emergence as a socially identifiable group dates from the late Heian period (the mid-twelfth century). From that time until the beginning of Japan's emergence as a modern state (1868), the samurai ruled Japan for close to 800 years. Over this period their worldview and their code of conduct naturally underwent change.

The purpose of this chapter is to describe bushido by relating historical episodes that took place in four distinct periods: the late Heian, Kamakura, Warring States, and Tokugawa.

LATE HEIAN PERIOD (MID- TO LATE TWELFTH CENTURY)

This period witnessed the development of the first code of conduct for the samurai, "those who bear the bow and arrow" (*yumiya toru mi no narai*).[27] The bow and arrow were the major weapons of the samurai (also referred to as *mononobe* and *bushi*) of this time. Throughout this period the supreme virtue among samurai retainers was loyalty; among their lords, benevolence. These two complementary virtues cemented a lord-retainer relationship more powerful than that of blood kinship. Indeed, it was expected that the samurai's family itself would be sacrificed if necessary in the defense of the lord and his family. For example, the samurai of the Genji clan existed to perpetuate the Genji, not their own families. Moreover, what mattered more than the samurai's family itself was the honor of the samurai's family tradition. For the individual, honorable death was preferable to living a dishonorable life. The code of self-sacrifice was not limited to actual combatants, but extended to women as well.

In 1150, the imperial succession was decided by a battle commonly referred to as the Hogen-no-ran. During that battle, Minamoto Yoshitomo (a Genji) suffered defeat and was killed. His young son Otowaka was captured and executed. According to a story in the *Tales of Hogen*, these are the words of one of the child's ladies-in-waiting:

> Never had I parted from this infant, never had I not thought of this infant. My thoughts were always with him, not even being aware of my own advancing age—always hoping for the day that he would become a lord. Painful is it to see him preparing himself for the execution. The

thoughts of my combing his hair, of letting him sit on my lap, his innocent face when asleep, and his sweet voice telling me that he would offer me the riches of the land when he becomes the lord swept through my mind as the time of execution approached. How can I continue to live? Who would guide him through the river of death, the valley of hells? To accompany him to death is nobler than to live in agony thinking of his uncertainty.[28]

Granted that land and property were the contractual bases for the lord-retainer relationship, the tie that bound them was not simply a business contract designed for mutual benefit, but one that intertwined the lives of the lord and his people, including the ladies-in-waiting. Of course, actual combatants followed their lord to battle and reaped the consequences, whatever they might be; survivors of lost battles frequently committed *seppuku* (better known in the West as *harakiri*, a vulgar expression), that is, self-disembowelment. It is this kind of spiritual tie—of love, loyalty, and dedication—that bound lord and retainer. The samurai who did not demonstrate such loyalty was referred to as a "man with two hearts." Dual loyalty was frowned upon.

There is of course no way to ascertain whether the passage taken from the *Tales of Hogen* is fact or fiction, but the fact that this episode is a part of the Japanese literary tradition and has been read through the centuries does indicate that the Japanese were deeply impressed by episodes of this kind. Nor is this an isolated case. In the sea battle of Dan-no-ura in 1185, the battle that sealed the fate of the Heike, Lady Tokiko, followed by all her ladies-in-waiting, plunged into the sea, Tokiko holding the infant Emperor Antoku. It was clearly an ancient custom to be prepared to lay down one's life for one's lord: to disembowel oneself in the case of a man or, for a woman, to drown herself or pierce her heart. Ladies-in-waiting always carried a dirk, concealed in their bosom and given to them by their mothers. Such were the virtues that characterized the conduct of "those who bore the bow and arrow" and their female companions, the virtues of bushido as it was forming at this time.

There was, however, a touch of compassion and, ironically, the constraint of duty that prevented exercising it during this period. At the Battle of Ichi-no-tani (1184), now a ward within the city of Kobe, Kumagai Naosane (1141–1208), one of the Genji leaders, was surveying the beach for Heike stragglers after having forced them out to sea. He found a Heike dressed in an officer's uniform, mounted on a horse, and heading out to sea. Naosane called upon him to return to land for a duel. The officer did, and a combat followed. Naosane overwhelmed the officer and pulled off his helmet to render the final kill. But to his dismay, he discovered a young man of sixteen or seventeen, about the same age as his own son, who claimed to be the son of the enemy's general, Taira-no-Atsumori. Naosane's men were now approaching, and Naosane had no alternative but to kill this young man. After the war, in 1194, Naosane shaved his head and became a monk, agonizing over the bind between the honor of a warrior and the tragedy that honor entails.

The Heikes, after having been defeated at Ichi-no-tani, retreated to Okujima (the present-day Takamatsu city in Shikoku), and thus began the battle of Okujima (1185). Nasu-no-yo-ichi (dates unknown), a Genji samurai skilled in archery, was called by his enemies and urged to hit a fan held by one of the Heike ladies on a boat, the outcome of which would reflect the pride of the Genji and would have a great impact on the morale of their samurai. He rode out to sea near the shore on his horse, successfully hit the waving target, and won the applause of both friends and foes. In the Western context, this incident might be said to have been a display of fair play. But in the Japanese traditional context, it is referred to as "the displaying of aesthetic value" (the term here means displaying "composure and grace" even at a trying time), attesting to the fact that aesthetic values were also honored by the samurai of this period, when wars were not mechanized. Hence, this episode is portrayed in *kyogen*, noh, and kabuki plays, all of which depict this kind of composure and grace.

KAMAKURA PERIOD (1192–1333)

The bushido of this period was referred to as the conduct of the warriors of Kanto (*bando musha no narai*), an area that included present-day Tokyo and its vicinity. The bushido of this period was built on that of the preceding period under the additional influence of three distinct historical circumstances.

First, Kamakura represented the government of the samurai, a type of government new in Japanese history. (The Genji and Heike warriors of the late Heian period were in themselves members of the aristocracy.) It had evolved as a challenge to the Heian aristocracy. The Kamakura samurai lived in simplicity, the Heian aristocracy in luxury. For example, the Kamakura samurai ate unpolished rice, dried sardines, root vegetables, pickled plums, and so on; the Kyoto aristocrats ate polished rice, processed foods, and sweets artistically arranged to please both eye and appetite. The Kamakura samurai's simple life and healthy diet, I would presume, were important factors in their political ascendancy.

The second was the Mongol invasions. That threat unified the Japanese under the Kamakura government, ruled by the Hojos, and fanned an intense nationalism. It was within the flames of that nationalism that Kamakura bushido reached the height of its popularity.

Third, this was also the period of the formal introduction of Zen. Zen attracted the interest of the Kamakura samurai and provided the philosophical basis for bushido. Bushido meant the willingness to face death, and facing death willingly meant conquering fear. According to Zen, fear can be conquered by eliminating the notion of self and thereby realizing the true self. Hojo Tokiyori (1227–63) and

Hojo Tokimune (1251–81), the oustanding samurai rulers of Kama-kura, were Zen practitioners.

Much has been said by historians about the impact of Zen on these two Hojo men. Hence, let us briefly describe the sociopolitical conditions that contributed to the decline of the Hojo power. Then, on that background, we can relate an episode that indicates the kind of bushido that emerged during this period.

Although the Hojos were able to repulse the Mongols, thanks in large measure to the "Divine Wind" (*kamikaze*, typhoon), neverthe-less, the Hojos were unable to reward the samurai because victory had secured no access to new land holdings. Taking advantage of samurai discontent, Emperor Godaigo (r. 1242–46) attempted to re-store imperial rule. Although he had the support of samurai leaders, such as Nitta Yoshisada (1301–38), Kusunoki Masashige (1294–1336), and others, the emperor was ultimately unsuccessful. From this chaotic situation emerged Ashikaga Takauji (1305–38). Takauji subsequently established the Ashikaga Bakufu (1441–91), a govern-ment that consisted of a loose coalition of the Kyoto aristocracy and provincial samurai. That coalition was destined to fail, for the aris-tocracy and the samurai had nothing in common. Thus the samurai eventually fought for power, and, taking advantage of the politically unstable situation, the peasants revolted. Both of these factors trig-gered the beginning of the Warring States period. The episode re-lated below took place during the waning years of the Kamakura Hojo regime.

Surrounded by mountain ridges on three sides and by an ocean to its south, Kamakura was an invulnerable site. Three passes over the ridges, however, connected Kamakura with areas beyond them: The Kobukuro, Kesho, and Gokuraku passes. Nitta Yoshisada was the commander of the imperial forces that attacked Kamakura. One of his forces attacked the Kobukoro pass. Akabashi Moritoki com-manded 60,000 defense forces at that site. According to the *Taiheiki* ("Chronicles of Wars"), intense battles raged for twenty-four hours, with sixty-five direct contacts made. By the end of that time, Moritoki's forces were reduced to 300. Taking full responsibility for his army's defeat, he committed seppuku. Ninety of his men followed suit. (A stupa exists today at this site honoring Moritoki and his men.) The remaining forces, however, retreated, reorganized, and managed to put up stiff resistance. Another of Yoshisada's forces headed toward the Kesho pass, which was less than 100 meters, but steep. Here again, the Kamakura forces put up a stiff resistance. Although fresh troops were alternately put into battle by the imperial forces, the Kamakura commanders urged their men to step over their fallen comrades, ignore the wounded, and charge into the enemy forces. Yoshisada's forces faced similar resistance at the Gokuraku pass. Eventually, though, overwhelmed by superior numbers, the Kamakura forces at these three passes were defeated, and their men without exception either fought to the end or committed seppuku to avoid capture.

Hojo Takatoki (1303–33) was the commander-in-chief of the Kamakura forces. When messages informing him of the defeat arrived, he too was ready to commit seppuku. At that time, Nagasaki Takaomo, one of his staff members, admonished him, saying that seppuku was still premature. With a handful of loyal retainers, he then charged into Yoshisada's forces with the intent of finding Yoshisada and having a duel with him. In that action he engaged in close combat over ten times and received thirty-three arrow wounds, but failed to find Yoshisada. He therefore returned to the side of his lord, Takatoki, exchanged his final drink of ritual sake with him, committed seppuku, plucked out his entrails and threw them in the direction of his enemies. He then calmly said to his lord that he would now lead him to the journey of death. Takatoki and his loyal retainers followed Takaomo. Thus ended the once-glorious Kamakura government in the year 1333.

WARRING STATES PERIOD (LATE FIFTEENTH TO EARLY SEVENTEENTH CENTURIES)

By the time of the Warring States years, bushido had taken deep roots among the samurai. This is the most colorful period of the samurai chronicles, its pages filled with men of humble birth challenging established powers with brawn and brain. Guns and explosives were introduced; no longer were battles fought between individual samurai as in the Heian period, but between armies. Battles progressed from firearms, to bows and arrows, to cavalry charges, and finally to hand-to-hand combat with lances and swords. Ninja were extensively employed as intelligence agents and experts in explosives, but the final assault was, of course, led by samurai skilled in swordsmanship. It was a period of violence, but it was that violence that colored the period with glory. To command the loyalty of the samurai, the daimyo of this period not only had to be great strategists but also had to demonstrate stability of character and be cultured and exercise benevolence. Uesugi Kenshin (1530–78) and Takeda Shingen (1521–73) were two such daimyo. The episodes related below, however, might have been a bit romanticized. Nonetheless, they do reveal an aspect of the samurai leaders' human character.

Kenshin rarely engaged in a battle designed for territorial expansion but eagerly responded to the calls of other daimyo whose territory was invaded. During battle, he commanded his troops without words, relying solely on gestures. Kenshin, surrounded by his banners and guarded only by a handful of retainers, remained calm. The fluttering banners surrounding him gave his troops confidence that their headquarters were secure and that Kenshin was in full command. Eventually, when Kenshin stood up from his command stool, the banners moved, indicating that the commander-in-chief was now ready for an assault. Riding in front of his troops, charging into the main body of his enemy, his troops followed their lord.

Kenshin honored silence and disciplined himself in Zen and Shingon Mikkyo. Silence and discipline commanded respect and trust. He repeatedly fought with Takeda Shingen, his traditional rival and one of the greatest strategists of the time. But their battles always ended in a draw. At one time, when the Imagawa-Hojo combined forces were in battle with Shingen and cut off Shingen's supply route, Kenshin sent his men to carry provisions to Shingen's troops. Kenshin believed that battles should be fought on battlefields, not by starving the opponent.

Shingen, like Kenshin, disciplined himself in both Zen and Shingon Mikkyo. He too felt that battles should be fought by the samurai on battlefields. Thus, when Oda Nobunaga attacked and burned the Hiei-zan Monastery, Shingen offered its monks sanctuary in his own territory. Shingen died unexpectedly in his early fifties. On his deathbed, he informed his son, Katsuyori, that among the numerous daimyo of the Warring States years, the only one who could be trusted was no other than Kenshin, his traditional opponent. When Kenshin heard of Shingen's untimely death, he went into deep meditation, paying homage to his lifelong opponent. It is this kind of daimyo, daimyo like Kenshin and Shingen, to whom the samurai pledged unconditional loyalty and thus contributed to their success.*

As the daimyo scrambled for power, loyalty remained the highest samurai virtue, but it was loyalty to an ideal rather than to an individual. If a lord proved incompetent, unworthy of the samurai's ultimate sacrifice, the samurai did not hesitate to abandon him and

---

* Of course, the success of daimyo during the Warring States period was also due to their access to economic resources as well. Both Kenshin and Shingen had access to gold and silver mines in their respective territories. Furthermore, these two men excelled in administering their territories militarily, politically, and economically. But after their death, their heirs failed to administer their territories as successfully as did their fathers. Takeda Katsuyori, Shingen's son, was defeated by Nobunaga in 1582, and Uesugi Kagekatsu, Kenshin's son, surrendered to Ieyasu in 1601.

search for another who was worthy. Furthermore, the samurai of this period had to combine courage with a gift for intrigue and betrayal. The Battle of Sekigahara, fought between the pro-Toyotomi (Hideyoshi died in 1598) and Tokugawa forces in 1600, is the historical setting that demonstrated these qualities.

This was the battle to determine the future commander-in-chief of all Japan—Tokugawa Ieyasu or Toyotomi Hideyori (Hideyoshi's son, who was only six years old). The Tokugawa forces were led by Ieyasu himself and the pro-Toyotomi forces by Ishida Mitsunari (Hideyori, with his mother, Lady Yodo, remained in the Osaka Castle). The Tokugawa forces consisted of 74,000 and Ishida's forces 82,000. The main forces of the two armies clashed at dawn on September 15. Although the battle was evenly matched during the morning hours, the Tokugawa forces began to prove themselves superior by noon. It was about this time that some of Ishida's forces—troops led by daimyo such as Kobayakawa Hideaki, Wakizaki Yasuhari, Ogawa Suketada, Akaza Naoyasu, and Kutsuki Mototsuna—betrayed Ishida, joined the Tokugawa forces, and provided them with a three-to-one numerical superiority. The Battle of Sekigahara ended with the Tokugawa forces' decisive victory by 2:00 PM. The turncoat daimyo, influenced by Ieyasu's behind-the-scenes intrigue and motivated by concern over their future security, determined the outcome of the battle. Ankoku-ju Ekei, a monk who was elevated to the status of a daimyo by Hideyoshi, and who was known for his constant preaching of the samurai virtue of conquering the fear of death, was a fence-sitter at this battle. After the battle, Ieyasu ordered one of his men to behead Ekei.

Although the pro-Toyotomi forces were decisively defeated in the Battle of Sekigahara, their headquarters in Osaka remained intact, and the Battles of Osaka in the fall (October through December) of 1614 and in the spring (April through May) of 1615 were to follow. The chief of staff of the Osaka forces was Sanada Yukimura (1567–

1615). The Osaka forces, protected by Osaka Castle, which was surrounded by moats, proved successful in the fall battle. Ieyasu called for a truce. Lady Yodo consented, overriding Yukimura's objection. During the brief moment of truce, Ieyasu had his men fill the moats. The following spring, he resumed the attack and defeated all the Osaka forces.

The drama of the spring Battle of Osaka stands in stark contrast to the intrigue and betrayal that characterized the Battle of Sekigahara. Fully aware that Osaka Castle had become a defenseless fortress, nonetheless, Yukimura and other ronin, such as Goto Matabe (1570–1615) and Ban Dan'emon (1567–1615), who had abandoned their pro-Tokugawa daimyo after the Battle of Sekigahara, gallantly fought against the numerically superior Tokugawa forces (200,000 versus 100,000), and died. Even today, Yukimura, Matabei, and Dan'emon—not personalities who have changed the course of history, to be sure—are honored by the populace as samurai who upheld moral justification at the cost of their lives.

THE TOKUGAWA PERIOD (1603–1868)

This period signaled a radical change from war and insecurity to peace and stability. Peace and stability, welcome as they were, had their dark side. The Tokugawa policy of isolation not only curbed the development of any progressive spirit but molded samurai into bureaucrats, who were meek and obedient to their superiors but rigid in holding their inferiors to the letter of the law. Furthermore, the centralization of the economy brought with it the development of urban values—a culture, as already noted, of merchants and city folk. Women dressed themselves in the ostentatious and impractical kimono with its meaninglessly long sleeves and heavy, delicately embroidered sash, which disguised their natural figures to the point of turning live women into dolls, and men sought entertainment in red-light districts such as the Yoshiwara. This culture was the setting for a dramatic case of samurai loyalty, which subsequently was made into a play well known in the West, the *Chushingura* or story of *The Forty-seven Ronin*.[29] The story goes as follows:

Asano Takumi-no-kami (1667–1701), the lord of Akaho in central Japan, was entrusted with the chore of entertaining imperial messengers at the Tokugawa Castle in Edo. He sought the advice of Kira Konosuke, a veteran official familiar with the proper protocol, but failed to present him with what Kira considered adequate gifts as tradition required. Kira misled Asano and humiliated him. Asano, a country lord and apparently a short-tempered man, drew his short sword in the castle (only short swords were carried within the castle) but succeeded only in inflicting a minor wound on Kira's forehead and shoulder.* Asano was condemned to commit seppuku, his territory liquidated, and his samurai retainers made ronin.

Oishi Yoshio (1659–1703), the chief councilor in charge of the Akaho Castle, surrendered it to the Tokugawa forces and disbanded the samurai, but managed to gain the support of forty-six men (plus Oishi, making a total of forty-seven). For the next year and a half, they lay low in the capital, disguised themselves as peddlers, or led lives of debauchery to lull Kira's suspicions while waiting for the chance to assassinate him. The assault on Kira's mansion, defended by scores of retainers, took place on December 15, 1702. It was a success. The forty-seven ronin placed Kira's head on Asano's grave at Sengaku-ji Temple in Edo, surrendered themselves to the Tokugawa authorities, and committed seppuku. This incident sent waves of exhilaration throughout the country: despite the fact that the forty-seven ronin were rebels against the establishment, they had proved, even at the time of peace and prosperity, that the spirit of bushido—loyalty and dedication—was still alive.

In 1868, just prior to the Meiji Restoration and, therefore, a time when the fate of the Tokugawas was about to be sealed, the imperial

---

* Asano was probably not a skillful swordsman. A skilled swordsman armed only with a short sword would not slash an opponent at close range, but instead would thrust his sword and penetrate it deeply using the weight of his own body.

army was dispatched against the samurai of Wakamatsu in northern Japan. The Byakkotai, a combat unit consisting of youngsters fifteen and sixteen years old, fought the numerically superior and better armed imperial army until Wakamatsu Castle fell. By then only twenty of those youngsters were still alive. Exhausted from battle and realizing the futility of further resistance, they committed seppuku to avoid capture and humiliation, although one survived. It is through this survivor that the details of the last hours of the Byakkotai is known. Although the Byakkotai were rebels, they were unanimously applauded by the citizens for laying down their lives for their lord and upholding the tradition of bushido.

Although intrigue and betrayal were qualities not alien to the samurai, nonetheless, the samurai's ideal virtue was bushido. And the bushido virtue underlying the episodes related above is consistent: the samurai chose honor over life.[30] Thus the three major features of bushido, all intertwined but focused on personal honor, are categorically described and interpreted below.

Bushido: Its Three Major Features

The first feature is loyalty and benevolence. Since the beginning of bushido in the Genji-Heike era, the concept of loyalty has varied: loyalty to one's lord in the Heian-Kamakura period; loyalty to a lord of one's choice in the Warring States period; and loyalty to one's immediate lord rather than to the central government in the Tokugawa period. But the common theme has always been loyalty and its demonstration by sacrificing one's own life. Thus the *Hagakure*, a samurai text composed in the early eighteenth century, says: "I have found the essence of bushido: one's willingness to die"[31] to preserve personal honor.

If the samurai must at all times be willing to lay down his life for his lord, the lord must then be worthy enough to command this kind of loyalty. He must have wisdom to formulate effective military strategy in war and political strategy in peace. And he must exercise benevolence. Benevolence means that a lord must trust his retainers at all times; delegate responsibilities unconditionally; not take credit for victory to enhance his own reputation, but instead honor those who carried out their duties and reward them for their merits; and not fault them at times of defeat, but accept responsibility himself.

Many medieval lords were greatly influenced by Sun Tzu's *The Art of War*,[32] a classical Chinese text on military strategy composed some 2,500 years ago. Unlike Clausewitz's military strategy or Machiavelli's political strategy (both of which emphasize system and organization), Sun Tzu's military strategy shows penetrating insight into human relations, focusing on the group. *The Art of War* is designed to formulate plans to mobilize a group of individuals into an effective force for the realization of a military goal. It is to the lord with this kind of ability that the samurai owed his loyalty.

The second feature is *gi*.[33] Etymologically, *gi* means "justice." It refers to the concept of doing what one conceives to be right, even if the action goes contrary to established law and order. Gi stems from an internal, personal concept of right and wrong, not one imposed from outside. Established authority recognized that law is not perfect: many times the samurai were caught between what was officially and legally right, and what was personally and honorably right. Hence the institution of seppuku, the most honorable way for the samurai to resolve this contradiction, testifying to the purity of one's motives. Seppuku is authority's response to personal gi. Thus the forty-seven ronin are also called *gishi* (*gi* + *shi*, the latter referring to the samurai), that is, samurai with a sense of gi—those who knowingly transgressed law and order and then without question accepted the decision of the state and committed seppuku.

The third feature is the aesthetic (here the term refers to the displaying of composure and grace even when one is faced with death) link between honor and death. This link was shaped by the traditional literary concept of *a-ware*, the feeling of the impermanence of life. Impermanence is a Buddhist concept, but the Japanese reinterpreted this concept by instilling in it a sense of pathos and romanticizing it as shown by sayings such as, "The flower of flowers is the cherry blossom; the samurai is the man among men" (*Hana wa sakuragi hito wa bushi*). The blossom and the warrior are all the more beautiful for the shortness of their lives. Hence, to die for honor is not only right and noble, but a way of making one's life a work of art, an art associated with tragedy. It is this element of tragedy as demonstrated, for example, by the Byakkotai—the perishing of young lives to maintain the purity of motive—that invokes the deep emotion of the Japanese familiar with the traditional aesthetic concept of a-ware.

Bushido's vision of personal honor, then, is more positive than the mere desire to avoid shame (see note 33). It is in fact deeply religious. Confucian thought influenced the Japanese concepts of loyalty and gi, and Shinto the aesthetic concept of a-ware. Thus, it is commonly held that bushido was institutionalized during the peaceful Tokugawa period under the influence of neo-Confucianisn and Shinto classics. True. But it is Buddhism that deals with the fundamental issue of existence: that which has form is subject to extinction, and that which has life is subject to death.

It was the samurai's view of existence that determined his view of life. That is, if he were to see death as something to fear, then his life with its constant possibility of death would be a source of endless anxiety. This was called "seeing death in the presence of life" (*seichu musho*). The way he faces death was therefore seen as a challenge put to him by life: this was called "seeing life in the presence of death" (*shichu usho*). The terms *seichu musho* and *shichu usho*— samurai expressions—were influenced by the Buddhist view of existence. It is the acceptance of this fundamental issue of existence— the impermanence of existence—and, more importantly, the positive response to it that shaped the samurai's view of life and drove them to preserve personal honor even at the price of death. (Life is impermanent, but honor is not.) Thus, a samurai's adage: "When a tiger dies it leaves its hide; when a man dies he leaves his honor" (*Tora wa shishite kawa o nokosu, hito wa shishite na o nokosu*).

But there is a streak of irony in bushido. Loyalty, gi, and aesthetic value may be honorable and inspiring virtues, but if unsupported by political insight, they are futile. Perhaps it was this sense of futility that prompted the samurai to develop a sense of pathos and to romanticize tragedy.

A *Critique of Nitobe Inazo's* Bushido: The Soul of Japan

Decades ago, as a teenager, I happened to run across Nitobe Inazo's *Bushido: The Soul of Japan*[34] (published in 1900) at a public library in San Francisco. At that time, already familiar as I was with kendo, I was deeply moved and read it several times from cover to cover. A more recent rereading has led me to take a broader perspective on the book's qualities and faults. To understand these, it will be helpful to know something of the author.

Nitobe was born in 1862 (six years before Japan's emergence as a modern state) as the third son of a prominent samurai family of the Morioka clan in northern Japan. His father died when he was six, and his mother cared for him until he was nine. At that age he was adopted by his uncle, Ota Tokitoshi, who was living in Tokyo. (It is to him that Nitobe later dedicated his book.)

In keeping with the intellectual mood of the period, his uncle persuaded him to study English when he was ten years old. At fifteen he entered the Sapporo Agricultural School, precursor of Hokkaido University, where he studied beside Uchimura Kanzo and others, who were to become prominent Japanese Christian intellectuals, and met William S. Clark (1826–86).

Clark was an American born in Massachusetts, a graduate of Amherst College, and a faithful Christian. He had risen to the rank of colonel during the American Civil War, and was appointed president of the University of Massachusetts in 1867. In 1876, he was invited to Japan to help in the development of Hokkaido, then a frontier territory. He was responsible for planning the educational curriculum of Sapporo Agricultural School and took the University of Massachusetts as his instructional model. He stayed at the school for nine months, teaching agriculture, botany, and English, and lecturing on the Bible at his home. He was a strict disciplinarian, took Christian ethics as his guilding principle, and prohibited any form of intoxicants on campus. Despite his short stay, he was highly successful in converting many young Japanese students to Christianity. His departing maxim, "Boys, be ambitious!" reverberated throughout Japan, stimulating the hopes and aspirations of many male students as Japan launched its ambitious modernization program. Clark left an indelible mark on Nitobe's thought.

Nitobe went on to study at Tokyo Imperial University, Johns Hopkins University, and in Germany. In 1890 he received his Ph.D. from the University of Halle. The following year he married Mary P. Elkington of Philadelphia, a Quaker who was to become Nitobe's lifelong assistant in the publication of his English book and essays. Nitobe returned to Japan in 1891 and taught at Hokkaido Imperial University, later at Kyoto Imperial University, and subsequently at Tokyo Imperial University. He was a faithful Christian, an educator, and a man who attempted to improve Japan's position in the world. But above all, the blending of his samurai background and his Christian convictions destined him to become a bridge between Japan and the West. His book, *Bushido: The Soul of Japan,* reflects this sense of self-imposed destiny. It deeply impressed Theodore Roosevelt, particularly after he witnessed the gallantry with which Japan, a newly emergent minor power, defeated the greatest land power of the time in the Russo-Japan War of 1904–05. It is said that Roosevelt went so far as to purchase a large number of copies and distribute them to his friends in Congress. The book was a synthesis of Nitobe's two worlds in which his samurai background and Confucian upbringing, and Clark's military background and Christian upbringing, blended without apparent difficulty. He saw no contradiction whatever between bushido and Christianity.

It is evident that the achievement of such a synthesis was personally important to Nitobe. After years of education in the United States and Europe, he was to become a distinguished international figure. But this involvement brought with it a need to clarify his own identity. Foreign affairs were dominated at that time by Europeans and Americans. Nitobe's Christian faith and his familiarity with Western civilization could not provide him with a clear identity. *Bushido* was evidently not only a work designed to introduce Japan to the West, but also a way for Nitobe to recover, reconcile, and introduce to the West the Japanese side of his own identity. It might be for this reason that he seems at times to apologize to his Christian friends: "Should any of my allusions to religious subjects and to religious workers be thought slighting, I trust my attitude toward Christianity itself will not be questioned."[35]

But Nitobe lived too long. Storms were brewing in the relationship between Japan and the United States in the 1920s when Nitobe was appointed Under-Secretary General of the League of Nations. In 1931, Japan launched a program of territorial expansion in Manchuria. Bushido became identified with militarism and nationalism. In the mind of Westerners, it was no longer the bushido that Nitobe had interpreted.

Nitobe's work, written in excellent Victorian English, is a collection of short, randomly organized essays in which he compares the virtues of bushido with their European parallels. This required considerable ingenuity and could only have been done by one who, like Nitobe, was knowledgeable in European history, religion, literature, and philosophy. The themes of these essays include the ethical system of the samurai, his courage, benevolence, honor, and self-control—virtues that are of course articulated in other cultures as well. Themes unique to the samurai are, however, covered in the twelfth section, "The Institutions of Suicide and Redress," and in the thirteenth, "The Sword, the Soul of the Samurai." These two themes are interrelated and deserve attention here, particularly in view of the fact that the episodes we have related previously dealt with ritual suicide (seppuku). Furthermore, these two themes have been selected as examples to indicate the flaws of Nitobe's work, as will be indicated in my comments that follow.

In describing seppuku, Nitobe presents vivid scenes taken from Mitford's *Tales of Old Japan*. A summary of two incidents related in that work follows:

Several years prior to the Meiji Restoration, a feudal lord and his large group of retainers were marching through Kobe. Two British men mounted on horses cut across in front of this group. Taki Zenza-buro, a loyal samurai in the service of the lord, commanded his men to fire, which was the law of the land at that time. The two British men were killed. The British counselor vigorously protested. In order to avoid war, the Japanese government condemned Taki and he was order to commit seppuku, to be witnessed by two Japanese officials and seven British officials. Taki appeared at the seppuku site, a Buddhist temple, bowed to the government officials of both countries, admitted his "guilt" and calmly committed seppuku. Behind him was the kaishaku-nin, not an executioner, but a friend of Taki. He beheaded Taki after Taki completed seppuku, the sign of coup de grace.[36]

This solemn account may be compared with another, also from Mitford and quoted by Nitobe, and even more poignant in its glimpse of tenderness within the constraints of duty, which reveals the strength of the samurai code even in a child. This story, apparently based on fact, centers around two brothers, Sakon, twenty-four, and Naiki, seventeen, who tried to assassinate Tokugawa Ieyasu to avenge their father. They failed, were captured, and condemned to commit seppuku along with their younger brother Hachimaro, who was eight. When the three were seated, the two older brothers told the younger one to go first. Hachimaro replied that because he had not yet seen seppuku he would like to see his brothers go first. He would then follow the proper procedure. Tears were shed upon observing their younger brother's calm in the face of death. They went first, followed by Hachimaro.[37]

Although the examples of ritual suicide presented above may indeed seem horrible, they are dramatic evidence of the samurai's calm in the face of death, and of their valuing personal honor over death, as Nitobe maintains. True. But to judge it by Western ethical standards, as did Nitobe, is to ignore the historical circumstances from which that tradition emerged. From this viewpoint, then, other questions arise: why did the samurai commit ritual suicide with a sword, and why does this form of suicide differ in form and context from that of the West?

The Western term *sword* may be translated by *katana* or *ken*, as in *kendo*. But the Japanese terms have quite different connotations. *Ken* is not simply a physical commodity, a tool of combat; it is also a symbol of the sacred, an extension of the "soul," to borrow Nitobe's expression. (I use the term *soul* in a commonsense, metaphysical context. Buddhism after all does not recognize a soul.) The manner in which the terms *sword* and *ken* are interpreted is symbolic of the difference betweeen Western and Japanese patterns of thought. The former is analytic, differentiating sword and man; the latter synthetic, integrating the two. Of course in Western arts, such as in music, painting, and so forth, the performer and the instrument used are also integrated. But the samurai carried this integration concept up to and beyond the point of death. What then is the underlying rationale of integration and synthesis as the samurai saw it?

A samurai was trained to defend himself and to kill his opponent with a sword; to do so, he was trained to realize not only body-mind integration but the integration of man and sword as well. That is to say, he had to make the sword an integral part of his body—indeed, a part of his *soul*. Furthermore, he knew the quality of his sword. Japanese swords are renowned the world over for their aesthetic as well as functional excellence. They were not mass produced (except for those made during World War II), but were individually crafted by hand through long hours of intense ritual tempering of the steel. One who is trained in swordsmanship, who appreciates the quality of his sword, is possessed by the sword. One who is possessed by the sword holds no fear of the sword. In this vision, seppuku signals the ultimate integration of body and soul. The sword is the agent of this integration. A samurai held his sword reverently, intimately, and fearlessly in the execution of seppuku.

The flaws in Nitobe's work, then, are that he did not place bushido in historical and cultural contexts and chose to justify it by drawing parallels between its virtues and those of medieval Europe. To evaluate an Eastern code of conduct from a Western standard is, of course, the flaw of his time.

5
The Modern Period

THE YEAR 1868 SIGNALED the beginning of a period of transformation of Japan into a modern state. It was brought about by dismantling the old sociopolitical system based on feudalism, by establishing a new sociopolitical system based on the West, and, ironically, by restoring imperial rule. The period 1868–1912 was ruled by Emperor Meiji. Hence, it is referred to as the Meiji period, and the earlier part of this period is referred to as the Meiji Restoration.

In 1869 the provincial lords surrendered their territories to the central government, which in turn established prefectural administrative units. In 1873 universal conscription was instituted, and males were drafted at age eighteen into military service. Military training was modeled on that of the West and made use of Western military equipment. The samurai, forbidden to carry swords and deprived of their lords and consequently of their income, were forced into commerce as employees or shopkeepers, enterprises in which most of them failed. Some of them, like Ken'kichi, commercialized kendo by giving public exhibitions. But although they aroused public interest for a time, they were destined to fail. These ex-samurai were not businessmen, and kendo was not a business enterprise. Thus in the early years of this transitional period, the early Meiji period, kendo barely managed to survive at private dojo.

Kendo in the Modern Period

In 1877, ten years after imperial rule was restored, Saigo Takamori (1827–77) led the ex-samurai of Kagoshima in southern Kyushu in a rebellion, popularly called the Seinan War.* The rebels were defeated by draftees—commoners—equipped with guns and cannons bought from the West. But despite their defeat the rebels, armed only with swords, proved extremely effective in hand-to-hand combat. Southern Kyushu, where Takamori lived and died, was the home of the Taisha and Jigen schools of swordsmanship.† Kendo after this

---

* The Meiji Restoration was brought about by a group of samurai. Although the leaders of this group were able to occupy prominent government posts after the restoration, the restoration itself produced at least 50,000 unemployed ex-samurai, with roughly 250,000 family members forced into poverty. These ex-samurai rebelled, such as in the case of Saga (the Saga Rebellion) in 1874, in Kumamoto (the Shinpuren Rebellion), and Fukuoka (the Akuzuki Rebellion) in 1876—all in Kyushu—and in Yamaguchi (the Hagi Rebellion) in the same year. Takamori's rebellion, the most serious one, took place in Kagoshima, also in Kyushu, in 1877. Saigo was an important figure in bringing about the restoration and was, therefore, an eminent statesman in the newly organized Meiji government. But disagreement with his colleagues led him to resign his post. He returned to Kagoshima where he established a military academy. Subsequently, urged by his students, he revolted. He disemboweled himself after his defeat.

† The Taisha-ryu was founded by Marume Kurando (b. 1540), a disciple of Kozumi Ise-no-kami, and was popularized in Kagoshima in Kyushu. *Taisha* means "to abandon"—probably, in this case, to abandon fear, doubt, and hesitation. The Jigen-ryu was founded by Zen'kichi, a samurai turned Zen monk, of whom very little is known. But his disciple, Togo Shigekata (1551–1643), who was first exposed to the Taisha-ryu, then studied under Zen'kichi, popularized the Jigen-ryu also in Kagoshima. *Jigen* means "revelation"—probably, in this case, to reveal the "true self." The Jigen-ryu is typical of combative swordsmanship: the first slash is the final and decisive one. Leaders of the government forces warned their troops to avoid the first slash of the Kyushu rebels. Nevertheless, it was reported that many of its troops were slashed, their own swords—used to defend themselves from the first slash—

was adopted as the primary training method for police officers, and skilled kendo practitioners were enthusiastically hired by police forces throughout Japan. This triggered a kendo revival.

The Great Japan Martial Virtues Association (Dai Nippon Budo-kukai), commonly referred to as the Budokukai, was established in 1895. It unified various schools of swordsmanship, standardized kendo forms, and issued ranks and titles to skilled kendo prac-titioners. Kendo was practiced at middle schools, vocational schools, teachers' colleges, and universities as an extracurricular activity. Kendo instructors were trained at centers sponsored by the Budoku-kai. But after 1913, because of its popularity, kendo training for school instructors was supervised by the ministry of education. By 1931 kendo was adopted as one of the physical education require-ments at middle schools and teachers' colleges.

The crash of 1929 and the worldwide depressions that followed brought national socialism to power and with it militarism. Japan invaded Manchuria in 1931 and North China in 1937. In response, the world boycotted Japanese goods and embargoed crucial indus-trial materials, which in turn further fanned Japanese nationalism and militarism, and ultimately led Japan to attack Pearl Harbor on December 7, 1941. After occupying the defeated nation, General Douglas MacArthur, the Supreme Commander of the Allied Powers (SCAP) in Japan, outlawed kendo and the Budokukai on the grounds that they had contributed to nationalism and militarism.

Only in 1952, the year when the U.S.–Japan peace treaty was signed, did kendo make a comeback. The All-Japan Kendo Federa-tion (Zen Nihon Kendo Renmei), following the Budokukai tradition, was established in 1953. From then on kendo practice was permitted in high schools and more advanced educational institutions. In 1957,

---

sunk deep into their own bodies. Jigen-ryu students were required to hit trees hun-dreds of times daily. Although primitive in its teaching method and lacking in style, it nevertheless proved itself to be extremely effective in hand-to-hand battlefield combat.

together with judo, it was reincorporated in physical education pro-
grams in middle schools and high schools. Today kendo is practiced
in dojo established in public and private schools, colleges and universities, police stations, and major corporations as well as in public and
private dojo.

To evaluate modern kendo, it needs to be classified into two general categories: professional and amateur. Further, the amateur category needs to be classified into subcategories: competitive and
recreational kendo.

Professional kendo is represented, for example, by Ogawa Chu-
taro, who was born in 1902 (and was still an active kendo master in
the late 1980s). His training curriculum involves forty-five minutes
of Zen meditation, chanting Buddhist-kendo precepts, and shinai-
swinging exercises, which are observed for at least three years prior
to putting on the bogu and engaging in combat practice. He was an
ascetic and probably the most respected kendo master of his time.
Because he devoted most of his time to training kendo students, I have
classified him as a professional. He transmitted the discipline, skill, and
rigorous training that characterized traditional swordsmanship.[38]

In contrast to Ogawa's kendo style is amateur kendo. Competitive
kendo is observed, for example, at dojo established in middle
schools, high schools, colleges, universities, and so forth. Rigorous
training is observed here also, but not to the extent of the Ogawa
dojo. After all, those practitioners have their own studies and profes-
sions to pursue. Recreational kendo is observed at private dojo where
the practitioners—children and housewives—assemble to enjoy
kendo, not as competitive sport but for recreational purposes.

Although each category has its own purpose and merits, my comments are focused on and limited to amateur competitive kendo, the
category that includes the great majority of today's kendo practitioners.

※   ※   ※

Tokugawa feudalism's system of hierarchy as a means to ensure law and order has had considerable impact on modern Japan. Thus, in kendo, rank-based rules of propriety dictate the conduct of its practitioners in the dojo, and seniority and order are strictly enforced. Rank, seniority, and order encourage formality and conformity, which are expressed in what is euphemistically called etiquette. The ranking system follows the *iemoto* tradition, known as *soke* in kendo, by which the governing institution—the All-Japan Kendo Federation today—delegates to its local centers the authority to issue rank certification and to collect the minimal fee. The ranking system as such does not need to be criticized, for there is nothing improper with a system that stimulates the development of skill; but the hierarchical tradition that underlies it too often encourages a despotic attitude among kendo instructors. Hierarchy and despotism of this sort are simply survivals from feudal Japan, against which many Japanese exposed to modern education cannot help but rebel. I am critical of a system of learning organized and standardized by a central authority (federation), a system that prevents individual creativity.[39] A mature instructor—an instructor who conceives of kendo as an educational process to realize personal growth—respects the rights of his students. He honors their need to progress as individuals and takes into account the creative nature of the individual.

Bushido in the Modern Period

It will be recalled that kendo discipline had its origin in the violent period of the Warring States years, and its way of life was institutionalized as bushido during the peaceful Tokugawa period. Hence, although kendo is a sport, underlying it is the bushido tradition developed in feudal Japan. It contains elements detrimental to the development of democratic society.

Let us take just one aspect of bushido and elaborate. The samurai's loyalty to his lord was demonstrated not only on battlefields but also by his willingness to commit seppuku upon the death of his lord, a practice known as *junshi*. Although junshi was outlawed in 1663, surprisingly, that tradition, or something like it, still held power over some military men in modern Japan—in the prewar period as well as in the period right after the war.

Emperor Meiji died on July 30, 1912. General Nogi Maresuke (1849–1912), the hero of the Russo-Japan War of 1904–05, after returning home from the emperor's funeral, dressed himself in ceremonial garb and disemboweled himself while his wife, Shizuko, pierced her heart beside him. Mori Ogai (1862–1922), a prominent writer of the time and a great admirer of Nogi, attended Nogi's funeral on September 19, and subsequently, under the impression of this ritual suicide, wrote the short story, *Okitsu Yagoemon no Isho* (*The Suicide Note of Okitsu Yagoemon*). In this story the retainer Okitsu Yagoemon slew a colleague in a fit of rage, but was forbidden by his lord, Hosokawa Tadaaki, to atone for it by disemboweling himself. Okitsu postponed his suicide until Lord Tadaaki's death and then followed his lord.

Not only the act but also its motive reflected the reality of Nogi's life. Nogi, fighting for the central government in the Seinan War, lost his regimental flag, assumed responsibility, and would have disemboweled himself but for the emperor's advice to refrain. With the emperor's death, Nogi evidently felt obliged to follow him and so repaid him for his benevolence. His life was his lord's.

Even in more recent times, on the eve of Japan's surrender to U.S. forces on August 15, 1945, some military officers disemboweled themselves before the imperial palace in Tokyo, and pilots plunged their aircraft into Tokyo Bay. Although Lt. Onoda Hiroo, most likely the last of the imperial army's stragglers, did not disembowel himself, he did refuse to surrender to his enemies for decades, finally emerging from the jungles of the Philippines and surrendering on March 10, 1974, twenty-nine years after Japan's surrender—and only after he was instructed to do so by his former commander.

In 1970 the writer Mishima Yukio, dramatically dressed in his own version of military uniform, disembowled himself at the age of forty-five. Speculation abounds as to his motive. Some say he had burned out his literary creativity and killed himself in depression. Be that as it may, on November 15, 1986, a memorial service was held for Mishima in the Chiyoda Public Hall in Tokyo, sponsored by such eminent personalities as Ishihara Shintaro, Uno Seiichi, and Hayashi Fusao. Hayashi, a right-wing writer, expressed the traditional perception of selfless suicide, announcing that it was love and concern for his country that led Mishima to his death.[40]

Although fanaticism, including the practice of junshi or something like it, is out of place in the modern world, it has been demonstrated publicly and frequently in recent Japanese history. Thus, already at the time of General Nogi's suicide, Natsume Soseki (1868–1916) and Akutagawa Ryunosuke (1892–1927), who, like Mori, were prominent writers of the time, rightly viewed Nogi's act as anachronistic. And recent critics claim that the ritual suicides of military men in 1945 and Lt. Onoda's refusal to surrender for close to three decades are eloquent testimony that elements of fanaticism rooted in feudal value concepts still hold power in the minds of some Japanese.

Mishima's suicide is a special case. Whatever his actual motive, and whatever the value of Hayashi's analysis of it, the statement that he was motivated by love for his country is misleading. It is an attempt by right-wing elements to glorify Mishima and to appeal to present-day Japanese by holding up the traditional ideal of gi—an ideal that is as alien to postwar Japanese reared in a democratic society as it is to Westerners. Even granting that he was motivated by a sense of gi, Hayashi fails to explain what Mishima conceived as personal honor and why that honor went contrary to established law and order. Mishima's disembowelment, then, cannot by any means be construed to epitomize the bushido tradition. His concept of bushido was, it is assumed, influenced by the *Hagakure* (the theme of which is "death is the essence of bushido"), a text that he greatly idealized but which has hardly any relevance to modern humankind.

Loyalty and the element of fanaticism associated with it enunciated in bushido will have to be channeled toward a higher cause, a cause beyond the confines of a hierarchically oriented feudal society. This essentially means that the premodern concept of bushido will have to be integrated with the disciplines of modern liberal education if bushido is to have any relevance and meaning today. Is this possible? Can the premodern bushido concept contribute to enhancing modern education? Because bushido essentially refers to a way of life shaped by martial arts, the specific issue to be discussed here is whether kendo training is compatible with liberal education.

Integration of Martial and Liberal Arts

The complexity of modern social organization paradoxically destroys the very fabric of individuality that has contributed to its formation. For example, emphasis on personal freedom, one of the major attributes of individuality strongly enunciated in a democratic society, inflates the ego to the extent that it makes demands without assuming responsibility. The kendo practitioner rejects this kind of individuality. This rejection does not mean commitment to some form of totalitarianism. It refers to the complete destruction of the ego that gives rise to mushin. Mushin is realized by disciplining the mind. In kendo, the mind is disciplined through intense practice, and this kind of practice provides the basis to discover the true self. The true self is that which has transcended the ego-clouded version of individuality and has realized the interdependence of self. Of course, individuality of this kind (the true self) is not completely lost in modern society. But it is gradually receding into the background from the pressure of organizational forces. Interesting though it may be, however, this is not the place to examine the modern human configuration shaped by the changing tide of history and by different cultural orientations. Suffice it to say that, today, personal growth is said to be shaped largely by education.

In 1964, Lyndon Johnson proclaimed education the major weapon in the war on poverty. But today school-age children are at serious risk of failing in school and society because of the high rate of delinquency, drop-out, and drug use. It is said, therefore, that there are 20 million functionally illiterate Americans today. Although educational policy, educational finance, and educational administration constitute important components of modern education, the basic ingredient of educational development is discipline. Thus, kendo, following the ancient samurai tradition, has developed the concept of integration of martial and liberal arts (*bunbu-ryodo* *). Donald Levine, a sociologist at the University of Chicago, therefore speaks of the synthesis of martial and liberal arts. He notes that,

> the very culture that originated and legitimized the basic conception of liberal arts we follow in the West supported at the same time a conception of martial training as an integral part of the ideal educational program, and moreover, the East saw this as a part of what can be called an Oriental Program of liberal education as well.[41]

The merits of cultivating both body and mind—following, to be sure, the classical Greek educational concept—have also been discussed by those in physical education, for example, by Richard Schmidt of the University of Nebraska.[42] In the Japanese tradition, bunbu-ryodo means that the learning of the classics (*bun*) and the practice of martial arts (*bu*) are like the two wheels of a cart: the cart (human beings) cannot be moved without the two wheels (*bun* and

---

* Bunbu-ryodo has its root in the eleventh century, the period when the Genji and Heike military clans emerged and when their leaders needed to be skillful in martial arts and cultured in order to command the respect of their retainers. Nonetheless, bunbu-ryodo was institutionalized in the Tokugawa period.

bu). Together, *bun* and *bu* enhance personal growth.[43] What then are the merits of this kind of education? Because Levine has already presented a curriculum proposal based upon the integration of martial and liberal arts,[44] three examples focusing on the issue of personal growth are presented.

First, although today's kendo instructors do not enforce an abusive practice of the kind observed in Tesshu's Shunpukan dojo, his concept of personal growth projects a distinct message even today. He instructed his students to suppress the ego, emphasizing personal honor rather than personal rights. Second, in kendo, there is no gender distinction. Both males and females practice together, although in a tournament, a female division may be provided for the benefit of the female. Nonetheless, kendo practitioners presuppose that its discipline is cultivated by both males and females. And third, perhaps most significantly, the lifespan of human beings has increased, thanks in large measure to the development of modern medical science; nonetheless, senior citizens are seeking quality of life rather than longevity. This quality is based on mental attitude and has nothing to do with age. Thus, many accomplished kendo instructors in their eighties are capable of intense practice and of training students over a half a century younger.* These men continue to realize personal growth throughout their lives, because they have developed the power of concentration through kendo discipline. The relationship between kendo discipline and aging is an intriguing subject which, it is hoped, will be investigated by qualified medical professionals.

Of course, this is not to say that kendo is the only form of sport that can contribute to personal growth. The discipline cultivated

---

* Some examples of men who have passed on in recent years but had continued to teach kendo in their eighties while active are Nakakura Kiyoshi, who taught at the Kozuka dojo in Tokyo; Oshima Isao, who was a public prosecutor and, at one time, the president of the All-Japan Kendo Federation; and Yuki Reimon, who was an eminent scholar of Buddhist history and philosophy and professor emeritus of Tokyo University.

through other sports can be implemented in the same manner. But kendo has a long historical tradition, during which time it was influenced by Buddhist thought. But, again, this is not to say that Buddhist thought is the only vehicle to enhance personal growth and that the educational system of Japan, a country where kendo is so popular, is the most effective. Far from it. Because of its long tradition, Buddhism in Japan represents a conservative institution in that it has lost the vitality it once had to stimulate cultural growth; and although the modern Japanese educational system has been successful in producing technocrats, it has been unsuccessful in creating individuals with its global vision that modern liberal education is designed to foster. What this means, then, is that the kendo practitioner needs to understand the shifting value concept from classical to modern kendo. We can no longer afford to adhere unconditionally to a value concept developed in feudal Japan and to reconstruct the human configuration developed during that time. How then is kendo taught at the University of Wisconsin–Madison, where kendo is a part of the university curriculum?

A course, Beginning Kendo: Integration of Martial and Liberal Arts, was incorporated into the physical education activity program of the Department of Kinesiology, School of Education, in 1989. Currently, enrollment is held to about forty students because of limited space. The class consists of lecture and practice. The lectures describe the Buddhist philosophical infrastructure of kendo, while practice exposes students to the fundamentals of kendo training, ultimately leading up to combat practice. The former requires a theoretical understanding of body-mind integration, the latter its experiential realization. Thus Dr. Julia Brown, professor emeritus and a past coordinator of the program, states, "That's what is often missing in education, because we traditionally have separated the person into mind and body and developed courses for each, as opposed to integrating the two."[45]

Although this course is housed in the Department of Kinesiology, it is regarded as an integral part of liberal education; and although it is modeled on the ancient form of bunbu-ryodo, it does not expose the student to a rigidly structured social order of the feudal period. Its purpose is to guide students to respond effectively to the challenges they will face in the near future—the challenges created by a society that produces a high rate of high school drop-outs, widespread crime, and drug abuse, which ensnare its citizens into insularity and prevent them from developing global vision. This course, therefore, encourages liberal education (the breadth requirement) under the supposition that it is capable of promoting global vision. Students who have taken this course have conclusively proved that they are willing to expose themselves to a discipline developed in a foreign culture and intelligent enough to understand kendo's value concepts—personal effort, personal responsibility, and personal honor. These kendo virtues, integrated with liberal education, I believe, constitute a new challenge facing modern kendo instructors in the United States, those who believe that kendo is not simply a utilitarian art of defending the self, but is a means to enhance personal growth.

Appendix
Ryu Lineages

Ryu lineages are difficult to trace for three major reasons. First, specialization in swordsman skills gave birth to various ryu. These skills were transmitted from master to disciple and were frequently not made public. That fact makes documentation of the history of ryu—the skill and way of life of the founders—very difficult. Second, creative disciples developed new ryu based on skills transmitted by their masters. Their creativity often obscured the skill of the original master. And third, ryu developed as the result of symbiosis. Bearing these issues in mind, historically ryu can be classified into three major categories.

Shinto-Buddhist Syncretic *Ryu*

Iazasa Choisai's Katori-ryu is a product of Shinto-Buddhist syncretism. Ryu in this category include Shinkage-ryu, founded by Kozumi Ise-no-kami; Shin-to-ryu, popularly known as Bokuden-ryu, founded by Tsukahara Bokuden; Kashima Shin-ryu, founded by Matsumoto Bizen-no-kami (1468–1524); and Ippa-ryu, founded by Morooka Ippa (sixteenth century). From Ippa-ryu developed the Tenpa-ryu founded by Iwama Koguma, Jiki Shinkage-ryu founded by Tsuchiko Doronosuke, and Mijin-ryu founded by Negishi Tokaku—all in the sixteenth and seventeenth centuries.

Kage-*Ryu*

Founded by Aishu Ikasai (1453–1538), this ryu was eventually transmitted to Kozumi Ise-no-kami, cited above as the founder of Shinkage-ryu. (The term *Shinkage-ryu* is probably derived from the Shinryu of the Kashima tradition, and the Kage-ryu of Aishu Ikasai. Details of the latter are unknown.) Marume Kurando (sixteenth century), Jingo Izu (sixteenth century), Hikita Bungoro (sixteenth century), and the Yagyu clan (sixteenth and seventeenth centuries) developed their own ryu based on the Shinkage-ryu tradition. (For details on Ikasai, see the footnote on p. 52.)

Itto-*Ryu*

The early history of this ryu is obscure. It was systematized by Ito Ittosai, if not in fact founded by him, in the late Warring States period. But because Ittosai studied under Kanemaki Jisai, who transmitted the Chujo-ryu, historians of swordsmanship claim that Ittosai transmitted the Chujo-ryu. Be that as it may, Ittosai's tradition was transmitted to Ono Tadaaki in the early seventeenth century, and in due time to Chiba Shusaku, Yamaoka Tesshu, and others in the late nineteenth century. But each of those men developed his own school.

The chart below shows some of the prominent schools and swordsmen arranged chronologically. (Asterisks under Comment indicate that although its founder is popularly known, the skill of its school and/or the history of its founder have been neither documented nor transmitted.)

Ryu	Century	Founder or Prominent Swordsman of that School	Comment
1. Kurama Hachi	mid-12th	Kiichi Hogen	*
2. Rinzaki	mid-13th	Taira Shigenobu	*
3. Chujo	early 14th	Nakashiro Deba-no-kami	*
4. Katori	early 15th	Iizasa Choisai	
5. Kyo	mid-16th	Yamamoto Kansuke	*
6. Shinkage	mid-16th	Jingo Izu-no-kami	*
7. Hikita Kage	mid-16th	Hikita Bungoro	*
8. Kage	mid-16th	Aishu Ikasai	*
9. Shinkage	16th/17th	Yagyu Clan	Different from 6 but of the same lineage
10. Bokuden	late 16th	Tsukahara Bokuden	
11. Itto	17th	Ito Ittosai	
12. Gan	17th	Sasaki Kojiro	
13. Niten Ichi	17th	Miyamoto Musashi	
14. Hokushin Itto	early 19th	Chiba Shusaku	
15. Shindo Munen	early 19th	Saito Yakuro	
16. Shinkage	early 19th	Shimada Toranosuke	Different from 6 and 9 but of the same lineage
17. Kyoshin-Myochi	mid-19th	Momoi Shunzo	
18. Jiki Shinkage	late 19th	Sakakibara Ken'kichi	
19. Muto	late 19th	Yamaoka Tesshu	
20. Tennen Rishin	late 19th	Kondo Isamu	

Although the chart indicates only what I consider some, not all, of the most prominent ryu, the following conclusions can be drawn. (a) The Katori-ryu is considered the first systematized school of swordsmanship because its tradition is documented. However, it is possible to assume that other ryu preceded the Katori-ryu, particularly those schools that developed in ancient Kyoto, collectively called the Kyo-ryu. This is a distinct possibility because swords and other weapons of very sophisticated nature were already used extensively in the twelfth century. Unfortunately, the records of those schools are not extant. (b) New ryu developed most prominently in the sixteenth and seventeenth centuries. And (c) Ryu were also founded in the nineteenth century. But the ryu developed during this period all have their roots in those developed in previous creative centuries, particularly the Itto-ryu. Modern kendo is a synthesis of a variety of ryu developed in the nineteenth century.

Notes

1. Joseph W. Elder says that sports include the following three components: (a) competition (with some "opponent"), (b) physical activity of some sort, and (c) established rules. See his "Social Changes and Evolution of Sport in America," in *Japanese Martial Arts and American Sports: Cross-Cultural Perspectives on Means to Personal Growth*, ed. Minoru Kiyota and Hideaki Kinoshita (Tokyo: Nihon University, 1990), p. 82.

2. Robert O. Ray, "Leisure, Aging and Personal Fulfillment in Contemporary United States," in *Japanese Martial Arts and American Sports*, pp. 98–9.

3. See D. T. Suzuki, *Zen and Japanese Culture* (New York: Pantheon, 1959), pp. 94 ff.

4. For details on Shinto-Buddhist syncretism, see Minoru Kiyota, *Gedatsu-kai: Its Theory and Practice (A Study of a Shinto-Buddhist Syncretic School in Contemporary Japan)* (Los Angeles-Tokyo: Buddhist Books International, 1982), pp. 23–40.

5. *Tenshin Shoden Katori Shinto-ryu*, Sahara, Japan: Comp., The Committee Commemorating the Six Hundredth Birthyear of Iizasa Choisai, 1987, p. 59.

6. *Tenshin Shoden Katori Shinto-ryu*, pp. 59–61. Also see Otake Risuke, *Katori Shinto-ryu* (Tokyo: Minato Research and Publishing Co., 1977), vol. 1, p. 16. (An English translation by the late Don F. Draeger is attached to this work.)

121

7. See note 4.

8. Kukai. *Hizo-hoyaku: Taisho shinshu daizokyo (The Tripitaka in Chinese)*, ed. and comp. Takakusu Junjiro et al. (Tokyo: Taisho Issaikyo Kankokai, 1924–34) (hereafter cited as "T"), 77.2426, p. 363a.

9. See Katsumata Shunkyo, *Mikkyo no nihon-teki tenkai* (Tokyo: Shunjusha, 1976), p. 149.

10. This theory is described in detail in Kukai's *Sokushin-jobutsu-gi*, T.77.2428. For English translations, see Hisao Inagaki, *Asia Minor*, new series, vol. 17, part 2 (London: Lund Humphries, 1972), pp. 190–215; Yoshita Hakeda, *Kukai: Major Works* (New York: Columbia University Press, 1972), pp. 225–35.

11. For Shingon Mikkyo's interpretation of *bodhicitta*, see Minoru Kiyota, *Tantric Concept of Bodhicitta, a Buddhist Experiential Philosophy* (Madison, Wisc.: South Asian Area Center Publication Series, 1986), pp. 2–11.

12. *Mahavairocana-sutra*, T.18.848, p. lc.

13. For details on the six elements, see Katsumata Shunkyo, *Mikkyo no nihon-teki tenkai*, pp. 158–64.

14. See David Edward Shaner and R. Shannon Duval, "Shinshin Toitsu Aikido as a means to Personal Growth," *Japanese Martial Arts and American Sports*, pp. 155–72. Here "body-mind" integration is referred to as *shin-shin-toitsu*.

15. *Katori Shinto-ryu*, p. 20. The origin of this term is unknown. It is a popular expression and is not necessarily Choisai's invention.

16. For details on the life of Takuan, see *Takuan osho zenshu* (Tokyo: Takuan osho zenshu kankokai, 1928); *Takuan zenji no kenkyu* (Tokyo: Daito Shuppansha, 1944). For its English version, see Dennis E. Lishka, "Buddhist Wisdom and Expressions as Art: The Dharma of Zen Master Takuan" (Ph.D. Dissertation, University of Wisconsin–Madison, 1976); *The Unfettered Mind (Takuan Soho)*, (tr. William Scott Wilson, (Tokyo-New York: Kodansha, 1986).

17. For an English version of *Fudo-chi Shinmyo Roku*, see *The Unfettered Mind*.

18. For an English version of the *Tai-A Ki*, see *The Unfettered Mind*.

19. D. T. Suzuki speaks of Zen as "Zen experience"; see his "An Interpretation of Zen-Experience," in *Studies in Zen* (Dell, n.d.), pp. 61–84.

Originally a paper delivered at the University of Hawaii in the summer of 1939, it appeared in *Philosophy—East and West,* edited by Dr. Charles A. Moore and published by Princeton University Press in 1944. Also, Shibayama Zenkei says, "The philosophical or dogmatic studies of *koan* are of secondary significance because the standpoint of such studies is fundamentally different from that of *true* Zen training, in which the only aim is to experience and live the *real* working spirit of Zen." See his *Zen Comments on the Mumonkan* (New York: New American Library, 1974), p. xiii. What these men are saying is that to cling to dichotomic thought (such as enlightenment vs. nonenlightenment) and remain fixed and frozen to one of them is a delusion. Zen experience, therefore, means to respond to the challenges brought about through dichotomic thought and to discover the true self, the self absent of the ego.

20. For an excellent study of the history of development of Japanese weapons, see Donn F. Draeger, *The Martial Arts and Ways of Japan,* vol. I, *Classical Bujutsu* (New York and Tokyo: John Weatherhill, 1973, 1981).

21. Miyamoto Musashi, *Gorinsho (A Book of Five Rings: A Classical Guide to Strategy),* trans. Victor Harris (New York: The Overlook Press, 1974). The term *Five Rings* is derived from Shingon Mikkyo's concept of five elements (see p. 28). Here, however, the term is used simply as chapter headings.

22. Sallie King defines the term *mysticism* as follows: "A religious experience [or mystical experience] is an extraordinary moment of awareness or transformation of awareness which subsequently alters one's mode of self-conscious being-in-the-world." "Buddha Nature Thought and Mysticism," in *Buddha Nature: A Festschrift in Honor of Minoru Kiyota,* ed. Paul J. Griffiths and John P. Kennan (Reno, Nev.: Buddhist Books International, 1990), p. 139. I will use this term later again with King's definition in mind.

23. For details on the Yagyu clan, see Tokunaga Shin'ichi, *Yagyu-ke no himitsu (The Secrets of the Yagyu Clan)* (Tokyo: Shirakawa Shoin, 1971). Classical records of the Yagyu family, such as the *Yagyu kyuki,* are available. But there is no comprehensive study on the Yagyu family in English. Nonetheless, translated works on the Yagyu-ryu are available. See Annotated References 29–31.

24. *Yagyu-ke no himitsu,* p. 56.

25. For a brief study on Yamaoka Tesshu in English, see John Stevens, *The Sword of No-Sword: Life of the Master Warrior Tesshu* (Boulder, Colo., and London: Shambhala, 1984).

26. Baelz contributed much to the advancement of Japanese medical science. His life and his view on the Japanese were published posthumously by his Japanese wife, based on Baelz's diary and entitled *Berutsu no nikki (The Diary of Baelz).*

27. For further details on the code of conduct for the warrior, see Uzawa Yoshiyuki, "The Relation of Ethics to Budo and Bushido in Japan," in *Japanese Martial Arts and American Sports,* pp. 41 ff.

28. Sagara Toru, *Koyo Gunkan, Gorinsho, Hagakure Shu* (Tokyo: Chikuma Shobo, 1969), pp. 6–7. *Tales of Hagen* is included in this work.

29. See, for example, A. B. Mitford, *Tales of Old Japan* (1871); G. J. Kohl, *Geshichten aus Alt Japan* (a German translation of Mitford's work) (1875); F. H. Junker von Langezz, *Segen Bringende Reissahren Midzuho Gusa I Vassallen Trueu, Chu Shingura* (1880); John Massfield, *The Faithful* (1915); John Allen, *The Forty-seven Ronin Story* (1972).

30. Ruth Benedict refers to Japanese culture as "shame" culture. See *The Chrysanthemum and the Sword: Patterns of Japanese Culture* (Rutland, Vt., and Tokyo: Charles E. Tuttle Co., 1959), pp. 222–27. Shame and honor are two sides of the same coin. Benedict emphasizes the former, the samurai the latter. What bothers me here is that Benedict seems to use the term *shame* in contrast to *guilt,* concepts that emerge from a Judeo-Christian value concept.

31. *Koyo Gunkan, Gorinsho, Hagakure Shu,* p. 215.

32. See *Sun Tzu: The Art of War,* tr. Samuel B. Griffith (London and New York: Oxford University Press, 1963).

33. Benedict translates *giri,* derived from the etymological root *gi,* as "reciprocal obligation." See *The Chrysanthemum and the Sword: Patterns of Japanese Culture,* pp. 141, 200, 211, etc. Gi is not simply a social obligation, at least not within the context of bushido. It is an internalized concept, and later ritualized as what Benedict refers to as a "social obligation" among the populace.

34. Nitobe Inazo, *Bushido: The Soul of Japan* (first published in 1900) (Tokyo: Teibi, 1912). Also see *The Works of Inazo Nitobe* (Tokyo: University of Tokyo Press, 1972), pp. 23–153. This work was translated into German (1901), Polish (1904), and Rumanian (1929).

35. *Bushido: The Soul of Japan*, p. 8.

36. *Bushido: The Soul of Japan*, pp. 94–7.

37. *Bushido: The Soul of Japan*, pp. 97–8.

38. For details on Ogawa Chūtaro's training method, see Tanaka Shizuo, "Problems of Character Formation through Kendo Training," *Japanese Martial Arts and American Sports*, pp. 62–4.

39. For another critical view of kendo practice, see Tanaka, "Problems of Character Formation," pp. 54–62.

40. This information was extracted from a pamphlet distributed by the Mishima kenkyu-kai commemorating the seventeenth anniversary of Mishima's death, dated November 1986.

41. Donald N. Levine, "The Liberal Arts and the Martial Arts," *Liberal Education* 70 (Fall 1984), p. 237.

42. Richard J. Schmidt, "Martial Arts, the Self, and Eastern Cultural Values," in *Japanese Martial Arts and American Sports*, pp. 189–204. Also see Frank C. Seitz, Gregory D. Olsen, Burt Locke, and Randy Quam, "The Martial Arts and Mental Health: The Challenge of Managing Energy," *Perceptual and Motor Skills* (1990), pp. 459–64.

43. A typical example of bunbu-ryodo training is that of the Nisshin-kan Academy of Wakamatsu that many teenagers, like the Byakko-tai members, attended. The Nisshin-kan was conceived of by Lord Matsudaira Katanobu in 1787—a period of affluence and easy life—to stimulate discipline, produce creative personnel, and inculcate pride. The curriculum consisted of reading Chinese and Japanese classics as well as training in a variety of martial arts. Granting that the curriculum was provincial and a far cry from what we now consider a liberal education today, it nevertheless contributed to personal growth by cultivating both body and mind. But the crucial issue here is that the Nisshin-kan educational policy made no status distinctions on the basis of students' family background, a significant issue considering the fact that the

academy was established during a feudal period. Furthermore, it promoted students according to personal achievement, not in terms of how many years a student spent in the academy as it is in today's Japanese college education. Most important of all, it presupposed that the discipline cultivated in martial arts can be applied in the study of the classics. For details, see Nakagawa Koi, "Nisshin-kan no kyoiku to Byakkotai," in *Aizu-Byakkotai*, comp. and published by the Rekishi Shunju-shuppansha, Aizu Wakamatsu (1987), pp. 33–41.

44. See Donald N. Levine, "Martial Arts as a Resource for Liberal Education," in *Japanese Martial Arts and American Sports*, pp. 173–87.

45. *Wisconsin* (January 30, 1994), p. 20.

Annotated References

Japanese

Many works on kendo technique are available. Five of the better ones are:

1. Ando Kozo, Nariki Fuminori, and Ozawa Hiroshi, *Kendo* (Tokyo: Taishukan, 1987). A well-organized book with excellent pictures. Designed for all levels of students interested in developing skills.
2. Hoshikawa Tamotsu and Edo Kokichi, *Kendo no Toreiningu* (Tokyo: Taishukan, 1987). A manual for training kendo practitioners written from the perspective of physical education. It provides precombat training methods and supports that kind of method by physical education data.
3. Mitsuhashi Shugo, *Kendo* (Tokyo: Taishukan, 1972). This work is primarily an instructor's manual, but it also covers the history of kendo and interprets kendo from the perspective of physical education.
4. Sato Nariaki, *Kendo: Seme no Joseki* (Tokyo: Sukii Janaru, 1987). This work is for advanced students. It provides skills for attack.
5. Yano Masanori and Okamura Tadanori, *Kendo Kyoshitshu* (Tokyo: Taishu Kan, 1979). A manual for the beginner, it deals with kendo skills in clear and precise language and contains excellent pictures and illustrations.

Swordsmanship is not merely the art and skill of manipulating a sword; it is also associated with military strategy and with bushido. Excellent classical works on these subjects include:

6. *Gorinsho.* Composed by Miyamoto Musashi in 1645. Musashi was one of the most popular swordsman of medieval Japan. This work deals with the skills and philosophy of the swordsman.

7. *Hagakure.* Dictated by Yamamoto Tsunasa and recorded by Tsuramoto Toshiro in the early eighteenth century. The central theme of this work is "Death is the essence of bushido."

8. *Koyo Gunkan.* Allegedly composed by Kosaka Nobumasa, an elderly retainer of Takeda Shingen (1521–73), the powerful lord of Kai and a renowned master of military strategy during the Warring States period. It was later revised by Otabe Kagenori (1572–1662). This work deals with military strategy.

Important sections of the above three classical texts have been collected, annotated, and rendered into modern Japanese:

9. Sagara Toru, *Koyo Gunkan, Gorinsho, Hagakure Shu* (Tokyo: Chikuma Shobo, 1969). The preface deals with the history of development of samurai thought. The appendices consist of a chronology of events related to important samurai figures and a well-selected list of references on Japanese military strategy and the history of bushido.

My work deals in part with Katori-ryu and Yagyu-ryu. Cited below are primary sources of these two schools:

10. Otake Risuke, *Katori Shinto-ryu,* 3 vols. (Tokyo: Minato Research and Publishing Co., 1977). It deals with the history and skills of this school interpreted by Otake and includes illustrations. An English translation is attached to each chapter.

11. *Tenshin Shoden Katori Shinto-ryu Kinenshi* (Sahara, Japan: Comp., The Committee Commemorating the Six Hundredth Birthyear of Iizasa Choisai, 1987). This work contains brief classical documents describing

the history, philosophy, and skills of the Katori-ryu with a modern Japanese translation attached. It also contains brief accounts of the history and lineage of other forms of classical Japanese martial arts.

12. Watanabe Ichiro, *Heiho Kaden-sho* (Tokyo: Iwanami Bunko Series 33–026–1, 1985). This is an annotated edition of the above work in modern Japanese.

13. Yagyu Munenori, *Heiho Kaden-sho* published in 1632. This work consists of three parts: Shinrikyo, Satsujin-to, and Katsujin-ken. The first is a manual on the Shinkage-ryu founded by Kozumi Ise-no-kami. The second and third parts are manuals on the Yagyu-ryu.

14. Takuan Soho, *Fudo-chi Shimmyo Roku*. This text was first presented to Shogun Iemitsu, who in turn presented it to Yagyu Munenori. It deals with swordsman skills, emphasizing the need to discipline the mind to develop skills.

15. Takuan Soho, *Tai-A Ki*. Whereas *Fudo-chi Shimmyo Roku* deals with swordsmanship, this work is designed to develop samurai character. It had considerable influence on the formulation of bushido in the early Tokugawa period. It may have been published after the above work, but the dates of publication of these two works are unknown. It is speculated that the two works were presented to the Shogun either in the late 1620s or early 1630s.

16. Takuan Soho, *Takuan Osho Zenshu* (Tokyo: Takuan osho zenshu kanko-kai, 1928). This is a collection of Takuan's work rendered into modern Japanese.

17. *Takuan Zenji no Kenkyu* (Tokyo: Daito Shuppan, 1944). A comprehensive work on Takuan and his works.

18. Tokunaga Shinichiro, *Yagyu-ke no Himitsu* (Kyoto: Shirakawa Shoin, 1971). A work dealing with the Yagyu clan.

English

Although books in English on the skills of judo, karate, and aikido are plentiful, works on kendo skills are not. The two books listed below are outstanding.

19. Junzo, Sasamori, and Gordon Warner, *This Is Kendo* (Vermont and Tokyo: Charles E. Tuttle Co., 1964). Both authors are skilled kendo

practitioners. Sasamori was a member of the Japanese House of Representatives and transmitted the Itto-ryu tradition. Warner is a former marine, studied kendo in Japan, and before his retirement was a faculty member of Long Beach State College. He now resides, I have been informed, in Okinawa. The book is well written and provides an adequate number of pictorial illustrations.

20. Hiroshi Ozawa, *Kendo: The Definitive Guide*, tr. Angela Turzynski (Tokyo: Kodansha International, 1997).

English works that deal with military strategy, samurai thought, and bushido are:

21. *A Book of Five Rings: A Classical Guide to Strategy*, tr. Victor Harris (New York: The Overlook Press, 1974). This is a translation of Musashi's *Gorinsho*, and, at one time, was extremely popular, particularly among corporation leaders.

22. *Budoshinshu*, annotated by Yoshida Yutaka, tr. by William Scott Wilson (Tokyo: Takuma Shoten, 1973; Burbank: Ohara Publications, Inc., 1984). An excellent translation of what the translator refers to as "The Warrior's Primer," a compilation of samurai thought.

23. *Bushido: The Way of the Samurai*, tr. Tanaka Minoru, ed. Justin F. Stone (Albuquerque: San Publishing Co., 1975). This is a translation of 4.

24. Cleary, Thomas, *The Japanese Art of War: Understanding the Culture of Strategy* (Boulder, Colo., and London: Shambhala, 1990). One of the best secondary works dealing with military strategy. It interprets the subject historically, culturally, and psychologically through careful research based on very difficult texts.

25. *Hagakure: The Book of the Samurai*, tr. William Scott Wilson (New York: Kodansha International, 1975). It is also preceded by an excellent introduction.

26. *Ideals of the Samurai: Writings of Japanese Warriors*, tr. William Scott Wilson (Burbank, Ca., Ohara Publications, 1985). A good selection of difficult but significant samurai writings, well translated and preceded by an excellent introduction based on good research. This work deals

with the thoughts of samurai, not with swordsmanship skill or the philosophy of swordsmanship.

27. King, Winston, *Zen and the Way of the Sword: Arming the Warrior Psyche* (Oxford University Press, 1992). An excellent work on the relationship between Zen and the samurai.

28. Ratti, Oscar, and Adele Westbrook, *Secrets of the Samurai: The Martial Arts of Feudal Japan* (Rutland, Vt., and Tokyo: Charles E. Tuttle Company, first edition, 1973; paperback, 1991). An excellent study of the discipline of the samurai.

29. Reid, Howard, and Michael Croucher, *The Way of the Warrior: The Paradox of the Martial Arts* (New York: The Overlook Press, 1991). An extremely interesting study of the samurai and his arts.

As previously mentioned, my work deals in part with Katori-ryu and Yagyu-ryu. For information pertaining to the former, see 10. Classical works on the latter are the writings by Yagyu Munenori (12, 13) and Takuan (15, 16, 17). They are available in English as cited below:

30. *The Sword and the Mind*, tr. Sato Hiroaki (New York: The Overlook Press, 1986). This work contains annotated translations of *Heiho Kaden-sho* (13.), *Fudo-chi Shimmyo Roku* (14), and *Tai-A Ki* (15). The translation is preceded by an excellent introduction, and the translation itself is well done. We are indeed indebted to the translator for making accessible these important primary sources on swordsmanship. Nevertheless, I doubt that the contents would be fully understood by a reader who is not a kendo practitioner of considerable experience. The *Heiho Kadensho* is particularly difficult, and Takuan's works may be somewhat esoteric to those who have not been exposed to Buddhist thought. The translator, however, is competent and obviously understood the contents of these works.

English works on Takuan are:

31. Lishka, Dennis Eugene, "Buddhist Wisdom and Its Expression as Art: The Dharma of the Zen Master Takuan" (Ph.D. dissertation, University of Wisconsin–Madison, 1976). A comprehensive study of Takuan

with an annotated translation of his major works, including *Fudo-chi Shinmyo Roku* and *Tai-A Ki*. It can be obtained from University Microfilms International, Ann Arbor, Michigan.

32. *The Unfettered Mind* (*Takuan Soho*), tr. William Scott Wilson (Tokyo-New York: Kodansha, 1986). An excellent study on Takuan and his thought written in good prose.

A work on Tesshu is:

33. Stevens, John, *The Sword of No-Sword: Life of the Master Warrior Tesshu* (Boulder, Colo., and London: Shambhala, 1984).

Excellent sources on the martial arts in general are:

34. Draeger, Donn F., *The Martial Arts and Ways of Japan: Classical Bujutsu*, 1st ed., vol. 1 (New York and Tokyo: John Weatherhill, 1973, 1981; *Classical Budo*, 1st ed., vol. 2. (New York and Tokyo: John Weatherhill, 1973, 1979); *Modern Bujutsu and Budo*, 1st ed., vol. 3. (New York and Tokyo: John Weatherhill, 1974, 1979). These three volumes offer the best available description of Japanese martial arts. The first is in two parts: *The Combative Rationale*, with a history of Japanese martial traditions, and *The Weapons and Their Use*. The second volume distinguishes between *bujutsu*, the classical martial arts of self-protection, and *budo*, the classical martial ways of self-perfection. Bujutsu gave rise to budo, as jujitsu did to judo and kenjitsu to kendo. The third volume describes the development of bujutsu and budo in the modern period, providing historical background to the emergence of modern Japan, inclusive of the prewar and postwar periods. The late Draeger, having studied under a variety of Japanese masters of martial arts (including Otake Risuke, the transmitter of Katori-ryu), was an accomplished master of Japanese martial arts in his own right. His work is a masterly description of the Japanese martial arts tradition of a kind perhaps unavailable in any other language at this time.

35. Draeger, Donn F., and Robert W. Smith, *Comprehensive Asian Fighting Arts* (Tokyo, New York, and San Francisco: Kodansha International, Ltd, 1980, 1985). This is a historical study of the martial arts throughout Asia. Japanese martial arts, including kendo, are discussed in chapter 4.

36. Herrigel, Eugen, *Zen in the Art of Archery*, tr. R. F. C. Hull (New York: Vintage Books, 1971). Herrigel was a German philosopher who taught in Japan after World War II, and there took up Zen meditation and Japanese archery. Although this book does not deal with kendo, I have cited this work because its central theme is body-mind integration, a theme articulated in Zen and applied in archery as well as in kendo.

I have made reference to samurai battles. An excellent source that briefly covers major battles is:

37. Turnbull, Stephen, *Battles of the Samurai* (London: Arms and Armour, 1987).

I have also made reference to Sun Tzu's *Art of War*. A good translation of this work is:

38. *Sun Tzu: The Art of War*, tr. Samuel B. Griffith (London and New York: Oxford University Press, 1963).

There is no comprehensive work on the Buddhist impact on kendo in English. The kendo concepts of mushin and body-mind integration are derived from Zen and Shingon Mikkyo, respectively. Buddhologists have written extensively on these schools. Kendo practitioners may find their books somewhat pedantic. But the work listed below might fulfill the needs of some kendo practitioners.

39. Shaner, David E., *The Bodymind Experience in Japanese Buddhism: A Phenomenological Study of Kukai and Dogen* (New York: SUNY, 1985). A good portion of this work is devoted to methodological issues, but the author demonstrates keen observations on the issue of body-mind integration theory as developed by Kukai of Shingon Mikkyo and Dogen of Soto Zen.

The Buddhist Yogacara school's concept of mind-onlyness has had considerable impact on Shingon Mikkyo and Zen and in turn on swordsmanship. For a succinct treatment of Yogacara, see:

40. John Keenan's introduction in *The Realm of Awakening*, comp., tr., and ed. Paul Griffiths, Noriaki Hakamaya, John Keenan, and Paul Swanson (New York, Oxford; Oxford University Press, 1989), 3–45.

A U.S.-Japan Conference on Martial Arts and Sports was held at the University of Wisconsin–Madison on August 7–10, 1989. Papers related to this work can be found in:

41. Minoru Kiyota and Hideshi Kinoshita, ed. "Japanese Martial Arts and American Sports: Cross-Cultural Perspectives on Means to Personal Growth" (Tokyo: Nihon University, 1990).

The popularity of martial arts in this country is attested to by the publication of the first issue of this respected journal in January 1992:

42. *Journal of Asian Martial Arts* I, no. 1, (January 1992). An excellent bibliography is attached to essays in each issue.

Glossary

ACALA   *See* Fudo.

ADHISTHANA   *See* Kaji.

AHIMSA   A Sanskrit term meaning "noninjury." The term first appears in the Upanisad, compiled between 600 and 300 BCE. Noninjury is also emphasized as one of the five basic precepts in Buddhism.

AIKIDO   A system of self-defense derived from the ancient form of jujitsu and systematized by Ueshiba Morei in the 1920s. Throwing and joint-locking characterize aikido. From Ueshiba's aikido emerged other schools, such as the Yoshin-ryu, Tomiki-ryu, etc. Though Ueshiba was an Omoto (a Japanese folk religion) follower, aikido is fundamentally based on yin-yang principles.

AIZU-WAKAMATSU   Aizu, located in the southeast district of present Fukushima Prefecture, was a feudal territory administered by Lord Matsudaira Katamori in the late Tokugawa period. In it was located Wakamatsu, the territorial capital. Tsuruokajo, the Aizu castle constructed in 1383, was located in Wakamatsu. In 1868, the Wakamatsu samurai (the remnants of the pro-Tokugawa forces) defended themselves against the imperial army equipped with superior weapons but were defeated. This battle produced the Byakkotai.

AKAHO   Also pronounced "Akoo," currently a city in Hyogo Prefecture, where the castle of the forty-seven ronin once stood.

AKUTAGAWA RYUNOSUKE   1892–1927. A student of Natsume Soseki and a prominent writer of the 1920s, Akutagawa is the author of *Rashomon* and many other short stories. Committed suicide.

135

ASANO TAKUMI (NO KAMI)   1667–1701. Attempted to kill Kira Kozunosuke in Edo Castle because of humiliation. He failed and was forced to
commit seppuku on March 14, 1701. His loyal retainers—the forty-seven
ronin—took revenge on December 15, 1702.

A-WARE (PRONOUNCED A-WA-RE)   A Japanese literary aesthetic term
meaning sorrow, a concept derived from the Buddhist theory of the impermanence of all things.

BAKUFU   Literally, a military camp. The seat of government ruled by the
samurai, for example, the Kamakura Bakufu, Tokugawa Bakufu.

BANDO MUSHA NO NARAI   The code of conduct of the Kamakura samurai.

BO   Short staff.

BODHI   A Buddhist concept meaning enlightenment.

BODHICITTA   The enlightened mind, wisdom. In Shingon Mikkyo, *bodhicitta* is presumed to be inherent in all beings, and exists beneath the
realm of the consciousness tainted by greed, hate, and delusion. *Bodhicitta*, therefore, is referred to as the true self.

BOGU   Kendo protective gear. Although highly protective today, it was
originally designed in the early nineteenth century. Hence, the present
bogu is a product of development and refinement of over 150 years. A
prototype bogu, however, was developed in the mid-eighteenth century.

BOOK OF FIVE RINGS   See *Gorinsho*.

BUDO   Literally, the way of life of the practitioners of martial arts. The
"way" has a long historical tradition and a solid infrastructure based on
Buddhist philosophy, Confucian ethics, and Shinto aestheticism.

BUDOKUKAI   The first kendo association in modern Japan, established in
1898. It was outlawed during the postwar occupation period because SCAP
considered it to have been associated with militarism and nationalism.

BUJUTSU   Martial skills.

BUNBU-RYODO   Literally, the two paths of martial arts and literary learning. Actually, the term refers to the integation of martial and liberal
arts. The concept presupposes that both forms of art share a common
attribute—discipline—and that this attribute must be implemented in
daily life. This concept developed from a historical necessity: the need
to tame the samurai trained in warfare to cope with peacetime activities
of the Tokugawa period. But the historical root of this concept can be
traced to the earlier period of the Genji and Heike, when samurai leaders
were required not only to excel in the arts of war, but also to be cultured
to command the respect of their retainers.

BUSHI   Another name for samurai.

BUSHIDO   The way of the samurai, codified in the late Heian period and through the Kamakura period. It was faithfully observed during the Warring States years and was subsequently institutionalized by Confucian scholars and Buddhist monks during the peaceful regime of the Tokugawa period. Hence, the code varies according to historical periods, but its basic ingredient is personal honor and a willingness to uphold it even at the sacrifice of life itself.

BYAKKOTAI   An Aizu-Wakamatsu combat unit composed of youngsters fifteen to sixteen years old who fought against the imperial army. After the defeat of the Aizu-Wakamatsu clan, twenty survivors of this unit committed suicide to escape capture. Although rebels against the new government, they were, nevertheless, honored for upholding the code of bushido.

CHIBA SHUSAKU   1798–1855. One of the eminent swordsmen of the late Tokugawa period.

CHUDAN   One of the stances in kendo. In chudan, one places the shinai in mid-position, aiming at either the opponent's throat or between the eyes. It is the standard stance.

CHUSHINGURA   The theatrical designation of the forty-seven ronin.

CHU-TZU SCHOOL   A neo-Confucian school developed in Sung China. It emphasizes practical ethics and was conceived of as the standard of moral behavior in Tokugawa Japan.

CLARK, WILLIAM S.   1826–86. A devoted Christian and a colonel who fought in the American Civil War. He was appointed president of the University of Massachusetts in 1867. In 1876, he was invited to Japan to help in developing Hokkaido, a new frontier at that time. He was responsible for planning the curriculum of Sapporo Agricultural School, precursor of Hokkaido University, and is noted for inspiring students such as Nitobe Inazo and Uchimura Kanzo.

DAIMYO   A provincial lord in medieval Japan. The term came into popular usage during the Warring States years and was extensively used during the Tokugawa period.

DAITOKU-JI   Rinzai Zen headquarters in Kyoto, established in 1324.

DAIZEN NAGAIE   A manorial lord of the Yagyu hamlet in the eleventh century. The Yagyu clan claims Nagaie as its ancestral root.

DAN-NO-URA   The site where the decisive battle between the Genji and Heike clans took place on March 24, 1185. The Heike suffered a decisive defeat.

DEBANA   Kendo term, the equivalent of the classical kendo term *go-no-sen/gasshi-uchi*, meaning "counterblow."

DEJIMA   A manmade island created within the port of Nagasaki in 1636 to enable the Dutch to conduct trade.

DHARMADHATU-SAMADHI   *See* Mudra.

DO   The torso, one of the permissible targets to hit in kendo. It also refers to the torso protective gear.

DO   The "way," a term originally employed in Buddhism (*mudra*), meaning the "path." It is also used in Taoism (*tao*). In the context of the martial arts, it is used in contrast to jitsu. Jitsu refers to a skill; do to the way of life derived through the discipline cultivated through jitsu—thus the terms kenjitsu and kendo and jujitsu and judo. The evolution from jitsu to do reveals that many samurai were not only skilled warriors but cultured warriors as well.

DOJO   A Buddhist term meaning the site of enlightenment (*bodhimanda*). Now popularly referred to as a meditation hall, site of practice, etc. When used in the limited context of martial arts, the term implies that the hall is the site of cultivating discipline.

EDO   The capital during the Tokugawa period (1603–1868), now called Tokyo.

EDO YAGYUS   When Yagyu Munenori was appointed as the official instructor of swordsmanship and as the head of Tokugawa intelligence, the Yagyu clan was divided into two groups: the Edo Yagyus (the Yagyus living in Edo) and the Owari Yagyus (the Yagyus living in Owari).

EIGHT NOBLE PATHS   The eight paths of practice in early Buddhism: right view, right thought, right speech, right action, right living, right effort, right mindfulness, and right meditation.

EMPTINESS (SUNYATA)   A basic Buddhist term. The concept presupposes that phenomena are empty of an essence and that the emptiness of an essence enables phenomena to dependently coarise. As such, phenomena are not absolute. They are in a flux. Buddhism claims, therefore, that to cling to things that are subject to change is a delusion. In this context, emptiness is an "ontological" concept. But Shingon Mikkyo conceives of emptiness as the source of creation, symbolically represented by Mahavairocana, a personification of the cosmos. The purpose of Shingon Mikkyo is to realize integration with Mahavairocana. This school appealed to the samurai because the samurai were not interested in ontological concepts but in attaining a synergistic force.

FIVE PRECEPTS   The basic code of morality of the Buddhist: noninjury, nonstealing, no sexual misconduct, nonlying, and abstaining from intoxicants.

FORTY-SEVEN RONIN, EPIC OF THE (POPULAR TITLE IN ENGLISH)   The forty-seven ronin are also referred to as the forty-seven *gishi* or the Akaho *roshi*. The forty-seven ronin under the leadership of Oishi Kuranosuke successfully took vengence on behalf of their lord Asano, killed Kira Kozunosuke, and, following the law of the land, committed seppuku.

FUDO (ACALA)   A Shingon Mikkyo deity. Fudo actually is an ancient Indian deity, but is now more popular in Japan than in India. This deity symbolizes one who is not swayed by external phenomena and hence is immovable. Many samurai worshipped this deity to nurture the discipline of immovability—immovable by externals and thus capable of realizing a flow-state.

FUDO-CHI SHINMYO   Composed by Takuan, this text provides instruction for the samurai to develop swordsmanship skills by cultivating the discipline of immovability.

FUKURO SHINAI   Bagged shinai bound by leather, invented by Kozumi Ise-no-kami in the sixteenth century to prevent fatal injuries. It was popularized by the Yagyu school and is the prototype of the present shinai.

FUSSHA-TO   A technique discovered by Ito Ittosai. It means confronting opponents empty-handed with only the force of ki-ai and instant ma-ai reading.

GEDAN   The lower stance in kendo. *See* Shumoku-no-ashi.

GEKKEN   A former name for kendo.

GENJI   One of the major military clans in the late Heian period. Also known as the Minamoto.

GI   The samurai's concept of personal justice. The samurai willingly transgressed the established law if they conceived of that law to be contrary to personal justice. But in doing so, they submitted themselves to the authorities and accepted the consequences—seppuku.

GISHI   One with a sense of gi.

GO-NO-SEN   Counterblow. *See* Debana

GORINSHO   Miyamoto Musashi's major work on samurai skill and conduct. The work has been translated as *The Book of Five Rings*. But the term *five rings* is derived from the Shingon Mikkyo's truth-concept, i.e., the five elements—earth, water, fire, wind, and space. These elements are a symbolic representation of emptiness that Shingon Mikkyo conceives as the creative forces of the universe. This work, however, is not an exposition of the five elements. Following the literary tradition of the time, the "five elements" designation is employed as chapter headings. This work is a biographical essay of Musashi.

HAGAKURE   A samurai text dictated by Yamamoto Tsunasa and recorded by Tsuramoto Toshiro in the early eighteenth century. It claims that the essence of bushido is one's willingness to die at any moment and be at peace with death.

HAIKU   A short Japanese poem arranged in 5–7–5 rhythmic syllables, and by rule employing seasonal themes. It has its origin in the fifteenth century but was popularized in the Tokugawa period.

HANA WA SAKURAGI HITO WA BUSHI   Literally, "The cherry blossom is the flower among flowers, a samurai is the man among men." The implication here is that both are aesthetically appealing but perish instantly.

HARAKIRI   A vulgar term for seppuku.

HASSO   A kendo stance. In hasso, one holds the shinai in an upper position but near the shoulder, like holding a baseball bat. This stance is most effective when surrounded by opponents on four sides.

HATAMOTO   A samurai in the direct service of the Tokugawas in Edo.

HATTORI HANZO   An Iga ninja who served Tokugawa Ieyasu. By the time of Masanari, Hanzo's son, the prestige of the Hattori ninja group declined and the group dispersed. Hanzomon, a site bearing his name, is one of the historical cornerstones in present-day Tokyo indicating the site where he once lived.

HEIAN   The ancient capital of Japan, now known as Kyoto. It also refers to the period when the capital was situated there, from the early ninth century to the late twelfth century.

HEIHO   Also pronounced "hyoho." The term refers to martial arts in medieval and premodern Japan. But this term includes military strategy as well.

HEIHO   The principle of peace.

HEIJO-SHIN   Mental/emotional evenness. A Zen term meaning the absence of emotional swings. Applicable in kendo combat.

HEIKE   One of the major military clans of the late Heian period. Also known as the Tairas. Defeated by the Genji at Dan-no-ura.

HOJO   There are two eminent Hojos in Japanese medieval history, both military clans. The Hojos in this work (see Tokimune and Tokiyori) are of the Kamakura period, not those of Odawara of the late Warring States years.

HOKKAI-JO-IN The Japanese version of *dharmadhatu-samadhi-mudra*. A stylized hand gesture (mudra) used in Shingon Mikkyo to attain union with the cosmos and to realize a synergistic energy. This meditational hand gesture is also used in kendo to realize the same state.

HONSHIN A Buddhist term referring to the original state of mind, a mind not distorted by external phenomena.

I-AI Quick sword-drawing. This type of art originated in the late fifteenth century.

IIZASA CHOISAI 1387–1488. The earliest systematizer of martial arts and the founder of Katori-ryu.

IIZASA YASUTADA The current official transmitter of Katori-ryu, representing the twentieth generation removed from Choisai.

ITO ITTOSAI c. 1560–1653. Founder of Itto-ryu and the master of Ono Tadaaki.

ITTO-RYU Literally, the school of one sword, a term used in contrast to *Nito-ryu*, the school of two swords. Actually, the term refers to "one-slash school of swordsmanship," one slash being decisive.

JIGEN-RYU A school of swordsmanship whose root can be traced to the Katori-ryu. It was popularized by Togo Shigetaka in the sixteenth century in southern Kyushu.

JITSU *See* Do.

JO Long staff.

JODAN The upper stance in kendo.

JUBEI (YAGYU) Son of Yagyu Munenori and one of the most skilled swordsmen among the Yagyu clan.

JUDO One of the Japanese arts of self-defense. It evolved from jujitsu (like aikido), was systematized by Kano Jigoro in the late nineteenth century, and is referred to as Kodo-kan Judo. It specializes in throw, grappling, and groundwork.

JUJITSU Forerunner of judo and aikido. It developed into various ryu, such as Sekiguchi-ryu, Shibugawa-ryu, etc., in the early Tokugawa period.

JUNSHI Following the lord to death. This custom was observed among the samurai from very early times but was officially outlawed in 1663. Nevertheless, its tradition has been observed on some occasions, even in the modern period.

KABUKI A form of Japanese play popularized in the Tokugawa period.

KAISHAKU-NIN One who aides a samurai performing seppuku. A kaishaku-nin is not an executioner. He is likely to be a close friend or a disciple of the accused.

KAMA-E   Popularly referred to as stance, kama-e involves three elements: (a) physical stance, (b) grasping of ma-ai, and (c) concentration.

KAMAKURA   An ancient capital of Japan located near Tokyo. It also refers to the historical period of the samurai government of Kamakura, from the late twelfth to early fourteenth centuries.

KARATE   A system of self-defense, theoretically, without the use of a weapon. It had its origin in China, was introduced to Okinawa in medieval times, and then to Japan in the 1920s. The Okinawans, prohibited from carrying weapons, developed karate based on Chinese fist-fighting techniques to defend themselves from the Japanese Satsuma samurai in the early Tokugawa period. Thus, many schools of karate have their origin in Okinawa. But these schools eventually merged as part of the Japanese martial arts tradition, as can be seen by the fact that they enshrine the Kashima and/or Katori deities.

KASHIMA   One of the earliest sites of the founding of Japanese martial arts.

KASUGA SHRINE   The Shinto protective shrine of the Fujiwara aristocracy. Although its home shrine is located in Nara, its local shrines appear at various sites throughout Japan, where the Fujiwaras once had their shoen.

KATA   Prearranged form-practice.

KATORI   The earliest site of the founding of Japanse martial arts. Both Kashima and Katori are sites of Shinto shrines where early Japanese swordsmen, such as Iizasa Choisai and Tsukahara Bokuden, inspired by these deities, founded their schools. Hence, Kashima and/or Katori deities are enshrined in martial arts dojo in Japan today.

KATSUJIN-KEN   A term popularly used in the Yagyu school (used particularly by Yagyu Munenori) in contrast to *satsujin-ken*. *Katsujin-ken* means "life-rendering sword" and *satsujin-ken* "death-rendering sword." Actually, these terms refer to forms of stance and states of mind. *Katsujin-ken* refers to a kama-e without an intimidating nature, enabling the opponent to exercise his skill without reserve and eventually allowing him to realize the limits of his own skill. *Satsujin-ken* refers to an intimidating kama-e designed to overwhelm the opponent. Jubei, Munenori's son, however, claimed that the lofty ideal of katsujin-ken is realized only through the experience of satsujin-ken; after all, one needs to develop a swordsman's skill to be able to allow the opponent to exercise skill without reserve.

KEHO (KAHO)   Literally, "flowering method." Stylized swordsmanship/ kendo.

KEN   Also called *katana*. A sword.

KENDO   The way of the sword, that is, the way of life of those trained in swordsmanship.

KENJITSU   Former name for kendo.

KENPO   Former name for kendo.

KI-AI   A verbal formula emerging from body-mind integration and indicating the gushing out of a synergistic force. To this extent ki-ai is a mantra.

KIRA KOZUNOSUKE   See Asano Takumi.

KOTE   The wrist, one of the permissible targets to hit in kendo. Also refers to the protective wrist gear.

KOZUMI-ISE-NO-KAMI   1503–77. Also known as Kami-izumi Nobutsuna, the founder of Shinkage-ryu and the mentor of Yagyu Sekishusai.

KUKAI   774–835. Systematizer of Shingon Mikkyo.

KUMITACHI   Prearranged combat kata practice popularly observed in medieval and premodern periods. It is still observed among schools that transmit the classical martial arts tradition, such as Katori-ryu, Yagyu-ryu, Jigen-ryu, Maniwa-nen-ryu, etc.

MA   Space. A term used in both kendo and the tea ceremony. When used in kendo, it is referred to as ma-ai.

MA-AI   Spacing. The term used in kendo implies control of space.

MAHAVAIROCANA   Mahavairocana, the central deity of Shingon Mikkyo, is described in the *Mahavairocana-sutra*. Literally, it means the "Great Light." Mahavaicana is a light deity symbolizing what Buddhism refers to as emptiness, an "ontological" concept. But in Shingon Mikkyo, Mahavairocana is conceived as the cosmic, the source of creation.

MANTRA   An Indic term found in the Vedas. In the context of the Vedas, it refers to syllables in praise of gods. Mantra was prohibited in early Buddhism. It became popular in parallel with the development of Tantric Buddhism. In the context of the Vajrayana school of Tantric Buddhism, mantra refers to a verbal truth formula. Shingon Mikkyo follows the Vajrayana tradition in the use of mantra.

MA O TORU   A Japanese tea ceremony term meaning controlling space.

MA-ZUMORI   Ma-ai evaluation.

MEIFU MADO NI OCHIN   "To fall into the pit of hell," the implication here being that enlightenment is found in the pit of hell. This, however, is a samurai term influenced by Zen, which conceives of death as a challenge of life.

MEIJI PERIOD   1868–1912. The period of Japan's emerging as a modern state.

MEN   Literally, the head, one of the permissible targets to hit in kendo. It also refers to the head protective gear.

MIYAMOTO MUSASHI   1582/4–1645. Musashi was one of the most prominent swordsmen of the late Warring States years and early Tokugawa period. He is the author of *Gorinsho*, translated into English by Victor Harris in 1974 as *A Book of Five Rings*.

MONDO   A Zen term meaning a debate. A mondo does not permit one to beat around the bush. A response to the point must follow a question immediately and directly.

MOSHIN   A Buddhist term meaning delusion, a state of mind attached to externals that produces—using the samurai expression—"fear, frustration, and confusion."

MUDRA   A Buddhist term referring to a hand gesture symbolizing an aspect of truth. The mudra employed in Shingon Mikkyo and kendo is hokkai-jo-in (*dharmadhatu-samadhi-mudra*), symbolizing man-cosmos integration.

MUGA   A Buddhist term meaning no-self, the realization of the true self, the self not disturbed by external stimuli. *See also* mushin.

MUNENORI (YAGYU)   1571–1646. The fifth son of Sekishu. Munenori was the head of the Edo Yagyu clan, the official swordsman instructor for the shogun, and the head of the Tokugawa intelligence. Munenori, with the help of Takuan, transmuted wartime bushido to peacetime bushido.

MUSASHI   *See* Miyamoto Musashi.

MUSHIN   The mind of no-mind. It refers to a state of mind hidden beneath the conscious mind and not disturbed by external stimuli. The samurai emphasized mushin to realize the flow-state.

MUTO-RYU   Literally, no-sword school. The Yagyu school is also referred to as Muto-ryu. Muto-ryu does not provide means for defense. It requires one to instantly read the intent of the opponent, charge into the opponent just before the opponent commences the attack, and disarm him. Yamaoka Tesshu, although he transmitted the Itto-ryu tradition, also referred to his school as Muto-ryu.

NAGINATA   Halberd.

NATSUME SOSEKI   1867–1916. An eminent writer of the Meiji period who studied in England (1900–03) and briefly taught at Tokyo Imperial University. His works include *Wagahai wa neko de aru* (1905), *Bocchan* (1906), *Kusamakura* (1906), and others.

NIRVANA   Literally, blowing out passion. In early Indian Buddhism, nirvana was conceived of as enlightenment, a state realized only after death.

NITOBE INAZO   1862–1933. An educator who studied in the United States and Germany, taught at Kyoto Imperial University and Tokyo Imperial University, became the Under-Secretary of the League of Nations, and is the author of *Bushido: The Soul of Japan*.

NOGI MARESUKE   1849–1912. The hero of the Russo-Japanese War of 1904–05, Nogi, together with his wife, Shuzuko, committed ritualistic suicide, junshi, following the death of Emperor Meiji.

ODA NOBUNAGA   1534–83. One of the successful military commanders of the Warring States years, Nobunaga was assassinated by Akechi Mitsuhide, one of his generals, just prior to military reunification of Japan.

OISHI KURANOSUKE   The chief councillor of Lord Asano of Akaho and the leader of the forty-seven ronin who successfully took revenge on Kira Kozunosuke on December 15, 1702.

ONO TADAAKI   1565–1628. Formerly known as Mikogami Tenzen, disciple of Ito Ittosai, and the transmitter of Itto-ryu. His school is referred to as Ono-ha Itto-ryu. Together with Yagyu Munenori, Ono was one of the official instructors of swordsmanship for Tokugawas. This school has had considerable impact on the schools of swordsmanship developed in the late Tokugawa period, and hence, in turn on the development of modern kendo.

OTAKE RISUKE   The current head instructor of Katori-ryu.

PRAJNA   A Buddhist term meaning wisdom. But the term does not refer to intellectual comprehension—it refers to direct cognition. Specifically, it refers to insight into emptiness. But in the samurai lexicon, *prajna* is not conceived of as insight into an "ontological" concept. It is understood in a psychological context, that is, as muga and mushin.

RIGHT ACTION   The fourth item in the Buddhist Eight Noble Paths system. It means to live a "pure" life, e.g., not inflicting injury on others.

RINZAI (ZEN)   The Japanese version of the Chinese Lin-chi Zen. Rinzai was introduced to Japan by Yosai, also called Eisai (1140–1215), in the Kamakura period; since that time, it has had considerable influence on the samurai.

RONIN   A samurai without a master; a wanderer; an unemployed samurai.

SADDHARMA   Although the term is frequently translated as "wonderful, profound, or mysterious law," it actually refers to a synergistic force.

SAIGO TAKAMORI   1827–77. A member of the Satsuma clan and one of the prominent leaders of the anti-Tokugawa, pro-emperor factions of the late

Tokugawa period. After the Meiji Restoration, he advocated the occupation of Korea. His views were rejected by the new government. He then retreated to Satsuma and established a military academy to disseminate his political ideas and cultivate loyal students. In 1877, he revolted against the central government, an incident referred to as the Seinan War, was defeated, and committed seppuku at Shiroyama in Satsuma.

SAKAKIBARA KEN'KICHI   1830–94. One of the eminent swordsmen of the Tokugawa–early Meiji period.

SAKYAMUNI   c. sixth century BCE. Founder of Buddhism in India.

SAMURAI   A Japanese warrior, also known as a bushi. In early Japanese history, known as *mononofu*.

SANMITSU   A Shingon Mikkyo form of meditation designed to realize human-cosmos integration—physically, vocally, and mentally. This form of meditation presupposes that man is a microcosm of the universe and the universe a macrocosm of man.

SATORI   A term popularly employed in Zen and frequently translated as "enlightenment." Actually, the term means "knowing the true self."

SATSUJIN-KEN   *See* Katsujin-ken.

SEICHU MUISHO SHICHU USHO   The phrase means "seeing death in the presence of life and life in the presence of death." It is a popular samurai expression that views death as a challenge to life.

SEINAN WAR   *See* Saigo Takamori.

SEKIGAHARA   Site of the crucial battle fought between the Tokugawas and the pro-Toyotomi daimyo in 1600. This battle assured the Tokugawas as the future rulers of feudal Japan.

SEKISHU (SEKISHUSAI)   1529–1606. The patriarch of the Yagyu clan who transmitted Kozumi Ise-no-kami's Shinkage-ryu tradition. Father of Yagyu Munenori.

SENGAKU-JI   A Zen temple in Takanawa, Tokyo, where the forty-seven ronin are buried.

SEPPUKU   Ritualistic suicide by disembowelment observed by the samurai.

SHINAI   Bamboo sticks tied together and used in kendo practice.

SHINGON MIKKYO   The Japanese equivalent of Tantric Buddhism systematized by Kukai (773–835).

SHOEN   Manorial property of the Heian aristocracy.

SHOGUN   In full, Seii Taishogun, the supreme military commander, a title first offered to Minamoto Yoritomi by the emperor in the late Heian period. The Tokugawas also used this title.

SHUMOKU-NO-ASHI   A swordsmanship term referring to a gedan stance: shinai pointing to the floor, left foot forward, body tilt forward. In modern kendo this type of stance is discouraged because it prevents leaping speed. In classical kendo it is encouraged because it provides physical stability and the force to cut through.

SOKUSHIN-JOBUTSU   A Shingon Mikkyo term meaning human-Buddha integration. But because the central Buddha of the Shingon Mikkyo pantheon is Mahavairocana, not the historical Buddha, and because Mahavairocana represents the cosmos, human-Buddha integration actually refers to human-cosmos integration.

SONKYO   A kendo term, indicating respect. Before and after a match, the practitioner takes a sonkyo position, stooping down with knees bent, demonstrating respect to the opponent.

SUMI-E   A form of painting using Chinese ink muted into shades. Also known as *suibokuga*.

SUN TZU   Author of the classical Chinese book on military strategy, *The Art of War,* allegedly composed some 2,500 years ago.

SUNYATA   *See* Emptiness.

SUTEMI   Literally, "body abandoning." In kendo, it refers to a "go for-broke" attack.

TACHIKIRI SHIAI   Kendo endurance practice that lasts an entire day, three days, or a week, with breaks only for simple meals and sleep.

TAI-A KI   A samurai text composed by Takuan designed to develop swordsmanship skill through the application of Zen concepts.

TAISHA-RYU   A school of swordsmanship founded by Marume Kurando (sixteenth century), one of the leading students of Kozumi Ise-no-kami, and popularized in the southern part of Kyushu from the late Warring States period to the early Tokugawa period.

TAKEDA SHINGEN   1521–73. One of the eminent daimyo of the Warring States period.

TAKUAN (SOHO)   1573–1645. A Zen master and the spiritual mentor of Yagyu Munenori, author of *Fudo-chi Shinmyo Rolu* and *Tai-A Kai.* Munenori transformed wartime swordsmanship to peacetime swordsmanship under the instruction of Takuan.

TOKAI-JI   The Zen monastery in Edo established by Tokugawa Iemitsu for Takuan.

TOKIMUNE (HOJO)   1251–81. An eminent leader of the Kamakura Bakufu and a Zen practitioner.

TOKIYORI (HOJO)   1227–63. An eminent leader of the Kamakura Bakufu and a Zen practitioner.

TOKUGAWA HIDETADA   1579–1632. The second Tokugawa shogun.

TOKUGAWA IEMITSU   1604–51. The third Tokugawa shogun.

TOKUGAWA IEYASU   1542–1616. The first Tokugawa shogun.

TOKUGAWA PERIOD   1603–1868.

TOYOTOMI HIDEYORI   1593–1615. Son of Toyotomi Hideyoshi. Hideyori was defeated by the Tokugawas in 1615 and committed suicide in Osaka Castle.

TOYOTOMI HIDEYOSHI   1536–1598. Hideyori's father. A man of humble origin, Hideyoshi served Oda Nobunaga (1534–83). When Nobunaga was assassinated by Akechi Mitsuhide (1526–82), he successfully took revenge and placed himself as the supreme military commander of Japan.

TSUKAHARA BOKUDEN   1490–1571. One of the eminent swordsmen of the early Warring States period and the transmitter of the Kashima martial arts tradition.

TSUKI   Literally, a thrust. In kendo, a thrust to the throat is one of the permissible moves.

UCHIMURA KANZO   1861–1930. Son of a samurai of the Takasaki clan, Uchimura studied under William Clark at Sapporo Agricultural School, precursor of Hokkaido University, converted to Christianity in 1878, and studied in the United States (1884–88). He identified himself as a pacifist in the Russo-Japanese war (1904–05), subsequently showed disrespect to the emperor, and was charged with *lèse-majesté*. He is most famous for taking a firm stand against institutionalized religion and advocated nonchurch Christianity. Together with Nitobe Inazo, Uchimura was one of the leading intellectuals of the 1920s.

UKIYO-E   A school of Japanese painting developed in the latter half of the seventeenth century and popularized in Edo. *Ukiyo-e* depicts the life of the pleasure-loving Edo people.

UPANISAD   A collection of ancient Indian philosophico-religious texts, originally written in Sanskrit, and compiled in 600–300 BCE.

VAJRACCHEDIKA-PRAJNAPARAMITA-SUTRA   One of the Buddhist wisdom texts. *Vajraccedika* means the summit or peak; *prajna* means wisdom, that is, a wisdom derived through direct cognition; *paramita* means perfection, implying practice. The term therefore means "the sutra which explains the peak of wisdom through practice."

VEDA   A collection of ancient Indian sacred books which, together with the Upanisads, are regarded as the basic texts of Brahmanism. Whereas the Upanisads deal with philosophical themes, the Vedas deal with rites and ceremonies. They are believed to have been compiled between 2,000 and 500 BCE.

WAKAMATSU   *See* Aizu-Wakamatsu.

WAKIGAMA-E   One of the kendo stances, holding the shinai in the right rear, the tip facing the ground.

YAGYU   *See* Edo Yagyus *and* Munenori.

YAGYU TOSHIYOSHI   One of the representatives of the Owari Yagyu tradition. He revolutionized swordsmanship and laid a foundation for modern kendo.

YAMAOKA TESSHU   1836–88. One of the eminent swordsmen of the late Tokugawa–early Meiji period.

YARI   Lance.

YAWARA   A term now seldom used, it refers either to jujitsu or judo.

ZANSHIN   A kendo term meaning sustained alertness.

ZEN   A Buddhist meditational school that originated in China and was popularized in Korea, Japan, and Vietnam.

ZEN NIHON KENDO RENMEI   All-Japan Kendo Federation, established in 1953.

Index

Schools

Technical Terms

Texts